Contents

A Wisley Handbook

Conservatory Gardening

ALAN TOOGOOD

Cassell

The Royal Horticultural Society

THE ROYAL HORTICULTURAL SOCIETY

Cassell Educational Limited
Villiers House, 41/47 Strand
London WC2N 5JE
for the Royal Horticultural Society

Copyright © Alan Toogood 1993

First published 1993

British Library Cataloguing in Publication Data
A catalogue record for this book is available from
the British Library

ISBN 0-304-32026-9

Photographs by Bartholomew Conservatories (p. 1); Eden Conservatories
(pp. 11, 18); Photos Horticultural; Robinsons of Winchester (pp. 6,10);
Harry Smith Collection; Sunrise Conservatories (p. 9); Technical Blinds (p. 16);
Elizabeth Whiting Associates

Typeset by Litho Link Limited, Welshpool, Powys

Printed in Hong Kong by Wing King Tong Co. Ltd

Cover: Most conservatories would not blend easily with a
picturesque cottage, but here is the perfect match – a
traditional timber-framed design.
   Photograph by Elizabeth Whiting Associates
Frontispiece: A conservatory should appear to be an
integral part of the house, as in this example which sits
comfortably in the L-shape of the dwelling.
Back cover: Bougainvillea 'Miss Manilla'. Bougainvilleas
are among the most popular climbers for small
conservatories, producing colourful bracts in summer.
   Photograph by Photos Horticultural

Introduction

The appeal of conservatories is well-established. The warm scents of the conservatory, earthy and floral, the year-round display of colourful and often exotic plants, are a constant delight. With romantic and nostalgic associations and a unique blend of beauty and practicality, a conservatory makes a desirable extension to almost every type of house.

Today the conservatory is most often used as an extra living room, a 'garden room' well furnished with both plants and home comforts. But its use can be adapted in many ways, for example adjoining a kitchen as a dining- or breakfast-room, or linking two rooms.

Fashions come and go, and many turn full circle. Hence, as the 20th century draws to a close, conservatories are a Victorian feature, often in the Victorian style, which are enjoyed once more. The revival started in the 1970s, with many variations appearing in the boom period of the 1980s, and an increasing number of companies selling conservatories or conservatory-related products.

Many Victorians had large elaborate glass structures built on to their houses. The interior landscaping was often jungle-like with waterfalls, pools and rockwork and the latest plants to be brought back from the tropics and sub-tropics by intrepid plant collectors. Many of the plants introduced at this time proved to be hardy out of doors, but some, like camellias, benefit from the protected environment of the conservatory where their lovely flowers can be enjoyed to the full, undamaged by rain or frost. Conservatories were often used as places for entertaining guests and enjoying plants of all seasons, a function just as important to us today.

First decide on the use of your conservatory. Will plants and family have equal status, will it be a place mainly for plants, or, most likely perhaps, will the plants be there largely as a background to family life? Architectural harmony is essential. Conservatories can be designed to blend with any house style. There are the popular Victorian styles to choose from, and many others, one for every taste and every style of dwelling.

Colours do clash in nature! The pea flowers of *Chorizema ilicifolium*, a small evergreen shrub, light up the conservatory in spring and summer (see p.37)

Choosing and Siting

A conservatory is usually a once-in-a-lifetime investment. It is essential to be absolutely certain of what you really want and need when buying or even building. Take as much care in selecting a conservatory as in choosing a house; all the aspects should be considered in detail.

SUPPLIERS

There are a large number of conservatory manufacturers, so the first step is to see as many different makes as possible. Various manufacturers have show sites or showrooms, and sometimes share a site with a garden centre. Some suppliers exhibit at major flower shows such as the Chelsea Flower Show, providing an opportunity of seeing many makes in one day.

Manufacturers supply well-illustrated and highly informative brochures or catalogues that give an excellent idea of quality and models available. They also list any show sites.

Conservatory manufacturers vary in the service they offer. At the top end are those who are able to design conservatories from scratch – as an architect designs a house. Others at the top end supply modular conservatories formed from standardised units (modules) to suit customers' requirements, a popular way to buy a conservatory.

Still others offer a range of models that cannot be modified – the customer simply chooses the most suitable design and size.

QUESTIONS

Suppliers will be able to answer all your questions regarding buying and installing a conservatory. Consult their brochures first.

You will need to know if planning permission is required and whether the structure comes under building regulations. Some manufacturers can handle this on your behalf if necessary, and

---

Victorian styles are popular today, especially for older houses, and modern materials like uPVC and aluminium may be used in their construction

will supply plans and other information for submission to your
local authority.

However, planning permission may not be needed, as many
conservatories come under permitted development, especially if
they are small ground-level conservatories or are *not* sited on a
wall fronting the highway. Very large structures and those to be
erected on listed buildings or in conservation areas *will* require
planning permission. Liaise with the planning department of your
local authority when you have made a choice, but *before* you
place an order.

Check that the manufacturer is a member of the Conservatory
Association, which sets high standards that should be followed.

With advice, decide on a suitable base, and find out if the
manufacturer is able to construct it. If not, find a local builder,
having received the exact specifications from the supplier. The
base involves a lot of work — usually it is a concrete slab laid over
at least 4 in (10 cm) of hardcore, the concrete being a minimum of
4 in (10 cm) thick, with the edges thickened to a depth of at least
12 in (30 cm). This is covered with a damp-proof membrane,
followed by a 2 in (5 cm) deep screed of mortar.

Is a brick or stone wall needed for the conservatory? Many are
built on low walls, in the attractive traditional way (see p.12).

Check who will erect the conservatory. Many are erected by the
suppliers, or they may recommend an erection service. Many
conservatories are not suitable for DIY erection.

Other questions you will want answered:

- How long will it take to build the base?
- How long will you have to wait for delivery of the
  conservatory?
- How long will it take to put it up?

STYLES

The enormous range of styles and designs may at first bewilder the
newcomer. There is one simple guideline to making the right
choice: choose a conservatory suited to the period and style of your
house. It should appear an integral part of the dwelling house and
not look as though it has been added on as an afterthought.

Victorian-style conservatories (particularly in octagonal
designs) are extremely popular, and are offered by many
manufacturers. Victorian, Regency and Edwardian styles have
large rectangular windows. Georgian styles have windows with
small panes of glass.

A modern conservatory in aluminium alloy. Lean-to designs with low-pitched roofs are also an ideal choice for bungalows

Owners of town and city houses often favour the Gothic style with a pointed arched roof and windows, or a conservatory with a curvaceous ogee arched roof.

There are many stylish modern designs for contemporary houses, with large arch-topped (in timber-framed models) or rectangular windows, as well as those with aluminium frames and attractive curved eaves. Other designs are more angular and some have a low ridge, making them suitable for erecting on bungalow walls.

Many conservatories are of lean-to shape, while others stand away from the walls and have pitched roofs. They can be octagonal, square, rectangular, hexagonal, bay ended or combinations.

An appealing and more unusual idea is to build a conservatory around a corner or corners. Another is an elevated conservatory with access from an upstairs room, which some companies will design and erect.

All of these options are there: the best advice is to shop around thoroughly until you find a conservatory that really meets your needs and expectations and suits your home.

Don't confuse lean-to greenhouses with conservatories of similar shape. A greenhouse is not designed as a living area and should only be used for growing plants. A lean-to conservatory has a stronger framework and is generally of more substantial construction than a greenhouse.

Many conservatories, especially traditional styles, are built on low base walls, such as brick, and these should ideally match the house

MATERIALS

The choice of materials used for the framework includes: timber, aluminium alloy and uPVC.

Timber

Softwoods (from coniferous trees) are often used, particularly western red cedar. Hardwoods (from deciduous broad-leaved trees), including oak and, if you must, farmed, renewable maghogany, are used by some manufacturers of high-quality conservatories. Timber can be painted or left its natural colour to match the house. Timber blends into any situation exceedingly well but does need regular painting or preservation treatment.

Aluminium alloy

This modern framework material is well suited to contemporary houses. It is also possible to buy conservatories in aluminium that match the period and style of older properties. Victorian and other styles are available.

A heavy aluminium framework is used for conservatories (as

The alternative to building a conservatory on a base wall is to have glass to the ground, resulting in good light at floor level

opposed to a light framework for lean-to greenhouses) and usually it has a decorative finish, perhaps coated with white or brown polyester paint.

Aluminium alloy is maintenance free, needing no preservation treatment. The framework of some conservatories is insulated to reduce condensation, which is inclined to occur on cold metal.

Stainless steel

This is included in the framework by some manufacturers of high-quality conservatories because it is a very strong material, therefore an excellent choice for certain large structures. Like aluminium alloy it is completely maintenance free.

uPVC

This modern material is becoming increasingly popular for the framework. It is a good insulator, will not rot or corrode and is maintenance free, needing no painting or preservation treatment. It can be supplied in a variety of colours, including white or brown, or with a woodgrain finish. Conservatories in both modern and traditional styles are now available in uPVC.

Base walls

Many conservatories, especially traditional styles, are built on low walls, varying in height from approximately 18 to 36 in (45 to 90 cm). Ideally the base walls should match the house and can be built of materials such as bricks, natural walling stone or ornamental concrete walling blocks.

The base walls may alternatively be an integral part of the conservatory, being constructed of timber or aluminium as appropriate. Some conservatories are supplied with reinforced-concrete base walls, with various decorative finishes.

The alternative to base walls is to have glass to ground level, very often used in modern designs and available in many styles and designs. A plus is more light at floor level – desirable if you intend growing plants in tubs or pots on the floor.

GLASS

Today there is a choice of traditional single glazing or modern sealed double glazing. The advantages of the latter are well known: it drastically reduces heat loss from the building, so reducing heating bills, as well as muffling outside noise. It is much more expensive than single glazing.

Note that toughened safety glass conforming to British Standards is used in conservatories: do not settle for anything less.

However, the roofs of many conservatories are 'glazed' with twin-skin or triple-skin polycarbonate, which is shatterproof and a perfectly acceptable roofing material. Other conservatories have glass roofs. The choice is yours.

Yet another option with some manufacturers is glass treated with a transparent coating that protects the surface from the elements and keeps it looking good and easy to clean.

Always keep glass clean to ensure maximum light.

DOORS AND WINDOWS

Central double doors are popular, traditionally hung in period styles, or of the sliding patio type in modern aluminium conservatories. Positions and numbers of doors can usually be varied to suit you. One can also have single doors.

Security is a very important point that you must clarify with the manufacturer. Doors should be fitted with high-security locks, including the internal door that provides access between house and conservatory.

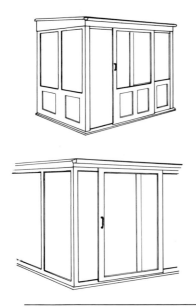

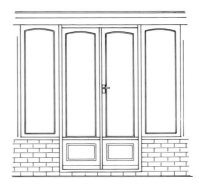

Figure 1: Modern conservatories may have sliding patio doors. Double central doors, traditionally hung, are often used in period styles

Many conservatories have opening windows in the sides. The more the better, as they can be used to prevent a temperature build-up during warm or hot weather. Ventilators in the roof are also essential to ensure a through-flow of air. Often one has the option of additional roof ventilators – again the more the better.

Remember that windows and ventilators must also be fitted with locks to deter burglars: it is useless having high-security door locks if acess can be gained through windows.

Door and window fittings vary in quality but should match the quality of the building. Brass fittings are often popular in the more expensive models.

A TOUCH OF STYLE

The more expensive conservatories, especially those in traditional styles, may be decorated with ridge cresting, dentil mouldings and finials in the appropriate designs. They may be made of wood, cast aluminium or fibreglass and provide a finishing touch to the outside.

SITE

A conservatory should obviously be erected on the best possible site. A very sunny position is preferable, but not essential, as success can be achieved in shade. Many plants enjoy or tolerate shade.

A conservatory is normally built against an outside wall, with access from one of the rooms of the house. This is not essential: if there is no suitable wall, it could be built against a garden wall, either a boundary or internal wall. As mentioned earlier, a conservatory can be elevated if desired, built on stilts or pillars, with access from a first-floor room.

Other points to note:

- Avoid covering an existing attractive feature of the house, if possible.
- Ensure that, from a technical point of view, a door can be created in the house wall.
- Building over a services inspection cover involves more complex base construction, and is best avoided, if possible.

Fit wire guards to the eaves of the house roof immediately above a conservatory to protect the conservatory roof from falling tiles.

The site does not necessarily have to be level. This can be adjusted during construction of the base. A base can be built on a sloping site but, of course, you will have to be prepared for much more construction work.

CONSIDERING THE ASPECT

If you do have a choice, site the conservatory in the sunniest spot available. A wall that faces south is ideal. Almost as desirable is a west-facing wall.

A conservatory sited on a shady or partially shady wall (one facing north or east), will be more expensive to heat, as the sun will not be much help. The 'atmosphere' will be different, too: a shady conservatory will not be quite so cheerful as one that receives plenty of sun. A bonus is that you are less likely to have to solve the problem of keeping the sun *out* to reduce temperatures.

It is highly desirable to site a conservatory where it is sheltered from cold winds. Wind results in rapid heat loss from a conservatory, particularly one with single glazing, which means it will be more costly to heat. If you really cannot avoid a windy site then at least opt for double glazing.

One of the worst sites is between two houses, as wind funnelling can occur, especially if they are quite close together.

Figure 2: Siting. A conservatory must not be subjected to wind or shade. Space between houses can be a wind tunnel. Windbreaks filter the wind

It may be possible to create a windbreak on the windward side of the site. A natural living windbreak, such as a row of conifers, is best if you have the space. Suitable subjects include the very fast-growing X *Cupressocyparis leylandii* (Leyland cypress) with grey-green foliage, or bronze-yellow in the slightly slower-growing cultivar 'Castlewellan'; *Chamaecyparis lawsoniana* (Lawson cypress), choosing strong-growing cultivars like rich green 'Green Hedger' or golden-yellow 'Lane'; or *Thuja plicata* (western red cedar) with shiny, deep green, aromatic foliage.

Keep the windbreak well away from the conservatory so that it does not cast a shadow over the building. Remember that a living windbreak will take a lot of moisture from the soil, and you really need a large garden for this idea to work well. One can put up an artificial windbreak, using windbreak netting, but this is unsightly, to say the least, and not recommended unless you can find a way of disguising it, say with climbers.

Avoid a site that is overhung with large trees as these will create a lot of shade and result in an accumulation of leaves on the conservatory roof and in the gutters. Rain will wash dirt and dust from the leaves of the trees and this could create grime on the glass. There is also the risk of falling branches damaging the conservatory.

A conservatory that is chosen in keeping with the house and sited with the above points in mind, will become visually harmonious very quickly.

Fixtures and Fittings

One of the most exciting stages of building a conservatory is fitting out the inside and turning it into a 'garden room' for use as an extra living room and as a place for plants. Features such as a suitable floor covering, furniture and blinds should be chosen to meet your requirements and to give the room its 'personality'. You must ensure adequate heating. As in any other room of the house, lighting and power points will be required. The electricity supply should be installed by a qualified electrician.

HEATING

Before choosing a heating system carefully consider the temperature you intend to maintain. If it is to be used as a living area, then maintaining a steady temperature of between 60° and 70°F (15.5° and 21°C) would be acceptable for most people. This is classed as a warm conservatory, which also makes an ideal home for many tropical and sub-tropical plants.

With a minimum winter night temperature of 50°F (10°C) you would have an intermediate conservatory, which also suits a wide range of plants.

The cool conservatory has a minimum winter night temperature of 40° to 45°F (4.5° to 7°C). This too will be suitable for a wide range of tender plants.

Intermediate and cool conservatories are, of course, rather chilly when maintained at the minimum temperatures, but remember they will often be warmer than this as the sun will raise the temperature.

The best idea, especially for a conservatory that is to be regularly used as a living area, is to run the central-heating system into it and install radiators, if this is possible. This is also the most economical means of heating the structure. However, plants need consistent warmth, so if your heating is turned off at night, you will need a secondary heating system, independently controlled.

Floor covering and blinds create the 'look' you want. Tiles are a sensible choice for both plants and people

Independent systems

It may not be possible to run the central-heating system into a conservatory, in which case one of the independent heating systems must be chosen.

Electric heating is highly recommended as it is efficient, clean, reliable, very convenient and automatically controlled. Make sure an electric heater has thermostatic control for economical running.

There are various types of portable electric heater that can be used in a conservatory, such as convection heaters and fan heaters. Alternatively you might like to consider storage heaters that run at night on cheap electricity.

If the conservatory is to be used primarily for growing plants and there is likely to be a lot of water splashed about, then it is highly recommended that an electric greenhouse heater is used. Again this may be a portable fan heater, or banks of tubular heaters mounted on the walls.

Gas and paraffin heaters are not ideal for conservatories that are also used as living areas, as they give off water vapour and this can result in a lot of condensation forming on the glass and framework, unless some ventilation is provided all the time the heater is in use. However, gas (natural or bottled) and paraffin heaters are suitable for plant conservatories, most of the latter being capable only of keeping a conservatory frost free.

Blinds, such as these attractive internal louvre side blinds, can be tailor-made and are supplied by many conservatory manufacturers

Obviously gas and paraffin heaters need more attention than electric heaters. Remember that paraffin heaters require more maintenance than any, and must be regularly cleaned, especially the wick, if they are not to give off fumes that are harmful to plants. Blue-flame paraffin heaters are recommended, used with high-grade paraffin.

Output of heaters
A heater must be capable of producing sufficient heat (its heat output) to maintain the minimum temperature required when the outside temperature is very low. Ideally it should have a higher output than needed to ensure it maintains the minimum temperature in periods of exceptionally severe weather.

A heater manufacturer or supplier should be able to advise on size of heater, given the size of your conservatory and the minimum temperature to be maintained.

FLOOR COVERINGS

The concrete screed will need covering, materials depending on how the conservatory is to be used. In the plant conservatory, the base could simply be sealed with a cement sealant. Or you could lay pre-cast non-slip concrete paving slabs for a more decorative finish.

For the conservatory that is to be used as a living room, a decorative floor covering will be required. There are tiles to choose from, including terracotta, quarry and slate. They are cool underfoot, but terracotta and quarry tiles helpfully come in 'warm' colours. Slate tiles are mainly grey, although some imported kinds come in shades of brown.

Non-slip ceramic tiles come in many designs and colours, so are ideal for creating a co-ordinated colour scheme. The same applies to vinyl floor tiles.

Cork tiles give a warm feeling underfoot and this natural product looks appropriate in a 'garden room'. Another natural material is woven seagrass floor covering with a latex backing.

If you prefer carpeting, then hardwearing cord is a good choice.

FURNITURE

As with floor coverings, choosing furniture such as tables and chairs is very personal. Some styles look more at ease in a garden room than others.

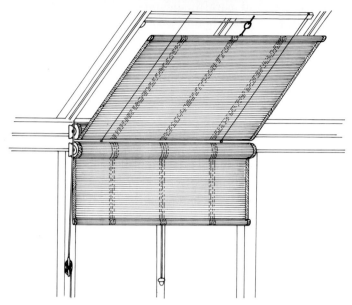

Figure 3: Traditional internal roller blinds can be tailored to fit the roof and sides of a conservatory and are made from various materials

If you like woven furniture, there is a choice of willow, rattan (a tropical climbing palm) and cane. Such furniture looks particularly good in traditional-style conservatories, as does wrought-iron furniture, or reproductions in cast aluminium.

For the modern conservatory, there is a big choice of wooden and tubular aluminium garden furniture, the latter often being plastic coated and well upholstered for comfort.

BLINDS

Note that, unless the conservatory is in a shady position, blinds are essential to shut out hot sun and thereby help to lower the temperature. Many people do not realise that the temperature inside a conservatory can become unbearably high when the sun is shining and blinds have not been fitted.

Blinds can be tailor-made and are supplied by many conservatory manufacturers. If possible, buy the blinds from the manufacturer of your conservatory. Most conservatory blinds are designed for internal use. Depending on the materials and systems, they are often available in a range of colours, so can be chosen to match the decor.

Traditional roller blinds come in various materials such as cotton and polyester fabric, fabric blinds metallised on the outside to reflect heat and glare, and glass-fibre fabric.

Alternatively there are louvered side blinds and retractable slatted or pleated roof blinds. Some come in polyester material. Another option is Venetian blinds, either manually or electrically operated.

Then there are the non-retractable louvre roof blinds in aluminium or cedar. The louvres open and close and can be operated electrically, manually or by various other control options. Versions exist for both internal and external use.

AUTOMATIC VENTILATION

Automatic ventilator openers, powered by natural heat, are highly recommended for roof ventilators. They can be pre-set to open at a required temperature and they close the vents again when the temperature drops.

Opening the side windows, doors and roof ventilators results in air movement or ventilation, but additional movement can be created with electric fans, such as extractor fans that remove stale air, or circulating fans that simply keep the air moving. Such fans are installed in or near the roof and are particularly useful during warm or hot still weather.

Now you are ready to consider in more detail the plants themselves. The variety and beauty of the plants you choose will create a living, always changing, picture within your home.

Figure 4: Roof ventilators can be opened and closed automatically by means of ventilator openers powered by natural heat

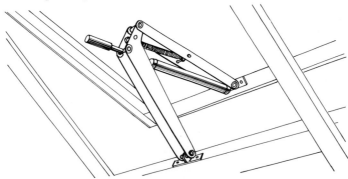

Preparing for Plants

To quote the original meaning, a conservatory is a structure in which tender plants are 'conserved' in cold weather. The writer John Evelyn first used the word in 1664. By the late 18th century the meaning had changed to a structure in which to display tender plants attractively and enjoy them. This is just as applicable today, when conservatories also provide extra living space, so we must devise various means of displaying them well.

DISPLAY STAGING

If you want to grow lots of small plants in pots, such as flowering and foliage pot plants, seasonal bulbs, and the like, you will need some staging to display them, unless you prefer to group plants on the floor.

Ideally the staging should match the conservatory: choose aluminium-framed staging for an aluminium-framed conservatory, or wooden staging for a timber structure.

Bench-type staging should be roughly at waist height and is usually placed against a side of the conservatory.

Tiered staging, with different levels, is more suitable for a conservatory, though. The tiers can be placed against the back wall, making good use of vertical space. Impressive and professional-looking plant displays can be created on this and trailing plants displayed to advantage.

One often has a choice of staging surface:
- Slatted allows good air circulation between plants, and heat can rise up through the slats.
- Gravel trays can be filled with horticultural aggregate which, if kept moist, will create humidity around plants.
- Water matting can be laid in the trays to provide capillary irrigation.

Aluminium staging is usually designed on a modular basis so that sections are easily added or removed.

Nerium oleander, an evergreen shrub flowering in summer and autumn, is available in various colours and ideal for large-pot or tub culture (see p.33)

Displaying temporary cool-conservatory plants like primulas, cinerarias, calceolarias and petunias in a group creates impact

Ornamental plant stands

Ornamental plant stands are alternatives, or additional to staging. The stepped designs are most useful in conservatories. Usually made of aluminium, they are especially suited to modern styles of conservatory.

SHELVING

While tiered staging helps to make the most of vertical space, shelving can take plants even higher. It might be useful on the back wall, for instance, for displaying trailing and cascading plants.

Shelving, including hanging types, can also be fitted in the roof area, if desired. Special greenhouse shelving is available and units consisting of a number of shelves, one above the other, are probably the most useful for display work.

RAISED BEDS

There is no doubt that permanent plants like shrubs, perennials and climbers grow very much better in soil beds as they have more root space. As the conservatory floor is concrete, it is most convenient to construct raised beds.

Beds can be built around the edge of a conservatory and, if space permits, in the middle. The shape is up to the individual – formal or informal. Importantly, avoid building against the walls of a conservatory as this will cause problems from damp penetration; so leave a gap.

Regarding building materials, aim either for a rustic look by choosing logs or natural stone, dry laid, or a more formal appearance with building bricks or ornamental concrete walling blocks.

To give plants a reasonable depth of soil and to prevent rapid drying out, build beds about 18 in (45 cm) in height. Remember to leave some drainage holes in the sides, at the base, if you are building with bricks or blocks.

Some rubble or shingle can be placed in the bottom and covered with rough leafmould to ensure good drainage, then the beds filled with good-quality light to medium topsoil.

After planting, mulch the beds with pulverised bark or, for a collection of cacti and succulents, with pea shingle or stone chippings.

The conservatory floor should be covered with concrete paving slabs, or terracotta, quarry, slate, or ceramic tiles, as drainage from the beds could make it damp at times. Alternatively, seal the cement screed. When watering, always be careful not to apply so much that it gushes out from the beds and floods the floor.

Figure 5: Raised beds will have a rustic look if built from logs or natural stone. A terraced bed gives greater scope for imaginative planting

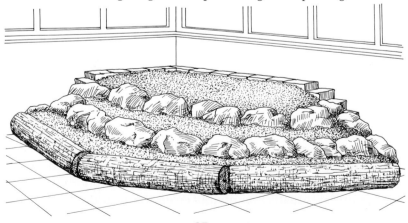

Alternative to raised beds

A simpler alternative to raised beds is large ready-made planters that come in various materials (the most common being plastic), sizes and shapes: the sort of thing that you see in hotel reception areas, restaurants and the like, containing impressive plant displays. These are watertight so there will be no problems from drainage. Group several together for a large planting area.

Another idea: instead of planting direct in planters, fill them with peat, a peat substitute like coconut fibre, or a horticultural aggregate, and plunge the pots to their rims. This makes for easy re-arranging of planting schemes.

SUPPORTS FOR CLIMBERS

The back wall of a conservatory offers an ideal location for climbing plants, but they will require additional means of support. Most simple is a system of horizontal galvanised or plastic-coated wires spaced 8-12 in (20-30 cm) apart. They can even be taken into the roof area. Wires can be secured with metal vine eyes screwed into the wall or timber framework. There are special plugs available for fixing wires to metal conservatory framework. All of these hold the wires an inch or two from the wall.

Alternatively fix trellis panels to the wall. There is a choice of wooden, plastic-coated steel or plastic trellis and panels come in various shapes and sizes. Fix them 1-2 in (2.5-5 cm) from the wall, using suitable brackets.

Moss poles

This attractive means of supporting climbing plants that produce aerial roots, like many of the philodendrons, can be inserted in pots, tubs or soil beds. Easily made, moss poles consist of a suitable length of broom handle or similar, enclosed in a cyclinder of small-mesh wire netting which is filled with live sphagnum moss. A small pot, inserted to its rim in the top, allows for easy moistening of the moss (which should be kept damp at all times) – simply fill it with water.

Wire-netting cylinders

Wire-netting cylinders of various diameters, supported inside with wooden stakes or canes, make excellent supports for ivies, which will eventually completely cover these supports.

Tropical foliage plants contrast dramatically in shape and texture in this warm-conservatory group, pleasing at any time of year

ELEVATED CONTAINERS

Many plants, especially trailing kinds, are effectively grown in elevated containers like hanging baskets. Choose the moulded-plastic type of basket with built-in drip tray.

Half baskets and wall pots, that are fixed directly to walls, are also ideal for trailers.

POTS, TUBS AND PLANTERS

There are many attractive containers for permanent conservatory plants, like terracotta pots and tubs, and concrete, reconstituted-stone and plastic tubs, in many sizes and styles. Up-market containers for conservatory plants, especially trees and shrubs, are square wooden Versailles-type tubs.

Then there are the self-watering tubs and planters, especially useful over periods when one is away from home.

If you wish to grow plants in normal flower pots, then consider placing them in ornamental pot holders, filling the space between the two with moist peat or substitute.

27

Plants are chosen to suit the minimum temperature of the conservatory. For the three temperature regimes refer to Heating, under Fixtures and Fittings (p.17).

The following is a very select list of plants suitable for growing in conservatories – there are many more excellent kinds available but lack of space prevents them being included here.

COOL CONSERVATORY

Permanent plants

Anigozanthos (kangaroo paw) Perennials that produce racemes of woolly tubular flowers in spring and summer from fans of sword-shaped leaves. *A. flavidus* (see p.31) has yellow-green flowers.

Suitable for pot culture, using well-drained acid peaty compost. Needs good bright light and sun, normal watering in summer, much less in winter. Liquid feed fortnightly in summer.

Bauhinia Evergreen, semi-evergreen or deciduous shrubs and trees that are grown for their flowers. Of the several species, *B. punctata* (syn. *B. galpinii*) can be recommended, an evergreen or semi-evergreen shrub to 10 ft (3 m) in height with bright red scented flowers during summer.

Grow in a pot or tub of well drained soil-based compost, or in a soil bed. Provide maximum light, water freely in the growing period, sparingly in winter, liquid feed fortnightly in summer, and thin out congested growth after flowering.

Camellia Evergreen shrubs with deep green shiny foliage and winter or spring flowers in shades of red, pink or white. Cultivars of *C. japonica, C. × williamsii* and *C. reticulata* are recommended. Also, scented cultivars are particularly noticeable under glass.

Grow in pots or tubs with ericaceous (acid) compost. Stand plants outside when flowering is over, choosing a partially shady and sheltered site, and re-house in autumn. Compost should be

---

Clianthus puniceus, above, is an ideal climber for the small conservatory as it grows only 1.8 m (6 ft) high; this is the variety *albus*. *Clivia miniata*, below, is an evergreen perennial which flowers best in spring and summer – if left undisturbed once planted or potted (see p.30)

kept moist throughout the year. Liquid feed fortnightly in summer. Provide plenty of ventilation.

Clianthus (parrot's bill) The species *C. puniceus* is normally grown, a 6 ft (2 m) high evergreen climber with pinnate leaves and, in spring and summer, clusters of bill-like red flowers.

Grow in a soil bed, or large pot of soil-based potting compost. Water sparingly in winter and liquid feed fortnightly in summer. Maximum light is needed, but shade from strong sun. Prune out growing tips in spring.

Clivia (kaffir lily) The evergreen perennial *C. miniata* (see p.28) has long strap-shaped leaves and during spring or summer produces heads of funnel-shaped orange flowers.

Ideally grow in a soil bed; alternatively in a pot of soil-based compost. Do not disturb once planted. Summer watering as necessary but in winter allow compost to almost dry out between waterings. Provide humidity in warm weather and shade from strong sun. Liquid feed fortnightly in summer.

Coprosma There are numerous species and cultivars of these evergreen shrubs and trees. Particularly attractive is *C. × kirkii* 'Variegata', a small dense shrub with white-edged leaves.

Ideal for pot culture, using well drained soil-based compost. Ensure maximum light, water freely in summer, sparingly during winter, and liquid feed fortnightly in summer.

Epacris Evergreen heath-like shrubs grown for their attractive tubular flowers produced in winter or spring. *E. impressa* (Australian heath) has pink or red flowers.

Grow in pots of well-drained acid compost high in humus. Provide sunny, airy conditions. Water moderately during growing season, very sparingly at other times. Flowered shoots can be cut back after flowering.

Hoya (wax flower) One of the most popular conservatory climbers is *H. carnosa* (see p.32), an evergreen to a height of 15 ft (4.5 m), but slow growing, producing white waxy flowers in pendulous clusters during summer, turning pink as they mature.

Grow in a soil bed ideally; alternatively in a pot or tub. Soil or compost should be rich in humus. In summer, humidity and shade from hot sun are appreciated, together with fortnightly liquid feeding. Water as needed in summer but in winter the growing medium should be allowed to almost dry out between waterings. Do not prune plants as they resent it.

Jasminum (jasmine) For fragrance there are few conservatory plants to beat jasmine. Try the white summer-flowering *J. polyanthum* and yellow-flowered *J. mesnyi* which blooms in

Anigozanthos, including the yellow-green *A. flavidus* (see p.29), are easily grown perennials flowering in spring and summer, provided the light is good

spring. Both these climbers are evergreen, reaching a height of at least 10 ft (3 m).

Ideal for beds, or pots/tubs of soil-based compost. Shade from strong sun and ensure plenty of ventilation. Water as needed all year round and liquid feed fortnightly in summer. To prune, thin out older wood in late winter and slightly reduce height.

Lantana The small evergreen shrub *L. camara* seems always to be in flower, producing rounded heads of yellow blooms which turn red as they age; or pink, red or white in its cultivars.

It will be more vigorous in a bed than if grown in a pot/tub of soil-based compost. Plenty of sun is needed together with airy conditions. In winter maintain the soil/compost only slightly moist. Liquid feed in summer. Prune by cutting back plants in

31

early spring, to within 6 in (15 cm) of their base. Renew plants regularly from spring or summer cuttings.

Lapageria (Chilean bellflower) The most popular conservatory climber is *L. rosea*. Growing to about 10 ft (3 m) in height, this distinctive evergreen produces sumptuous crimson waxy bell-shaped flowers during late summer and autumn.

It should be grown in acid humus-rich soil or compost, in a bed or large pot. Provide light shade from strong sun, airy conditions, water as needed all year round and liquid feed fortnightly in summer. Do not prune.

Metrosideros Evergreen shrubs and trees whose flowers, produced in winter, have numerous showy stamens. *M. excelsa* (rata, New Zealand Christmas tree), is a tree with shiny deep green leaves, white felted below, and flowers with crimson stamens.

Can be grown in a large pot or tub of well drained soil-based compost, or in a soil bed. Ensure maximum light, and water freely

Hoya carnosa is one of the most popular climbers for small conservatories, but a slow grower, producing waxy flowers with a heady scent during the summer (see p.30)

during the growing period (when fortnightly feeding can be carried out) but moderately at other times.

Nerium (oleander) The evergreen shrub *N. oleander* (see p.22) flowers profusely in summer and autumn, bearing clusters of purple-red, red, pink or white blooms, double in some cultivars.

Best grown in large pots or tubs as it relishes a spell out of doors during the summer. Grow in soil-based compost. Can also be grown in beds. Needs plenty of sun and airy conditions. Water as needed in summer; but, during winter allow soil/compost to partially dry out between waterings. Liquid feed fortnightly in summer.

Strelitzia (bird of paradise flower) *S. reginae* (see p.60) is an evergreen perennial with large banana-like leaves. Older established plants (at least five to seven years) produce a succession of striking orange and blue flowers in summer, in shape like a bird's head.

Grow in a soil bed or large pot/tub of soil-based compost. Likes plenty of sun and airy conditions. Water as needed in summer, but keep only slightly moist during winter. Liquid feed fortnightly in summer.

Temporary plants

These plants are flowered only once in the conservatory. When the display is over, either discard or plant in the garden, depending on type.

Calceolaria (slipper wort) Calceolaria hybrids are generally grown as biennial pot plants and are discarded after flowering. They produce colourful pouched flowers in shades of yellow, red and orange, often strikingly spotted, during spring or summer.

Seeds are sown during early summer and should not be covered with compost. Germinate in cool conditions, such as a garden frame. Prick off seedlings into trays and then pot into 3 in (8 cm) pots. Grow the plants on in the frame in airy conditions, shade from strong sun, and transfer to the conservatory in autumn, when they can be potted into 5 in (13 cm) pots. Pot into final 6 in (15 cm) pots in late winter. Soilless potting compost makes a good growing medium. Keep plants in cool and airy conditions at all times, shade from strong sun, and maintain the compost steadily moist but not wet.

Calomeria (Humea) The species *C. amaranthoides* (*H. elegans*) (incense plant) is grown as a biennial. It has an upright habit, to a height of 6 ft (1.8 m), and smells strongly of incense. The leaves are lance shaped and in summer and autumn the plant bears large heads of small pink or red flowers.

Sow seeds during mid-summer, and grow plants in pots of rich, well drained soil-based compost. Ensure sunny, airy conditions. Water freely during growing season, sparingly in winter but avoid wilting point, or wetting the foliage at any time. Liquid feed fortnightly in summer.

Chrysanthemum There are numerous types of chrysanthemum for flowering under glass, but the charm chrysanths make a marvellous show in the cool conservatory for very little effort on the part of the gardener. They are bushy plants about 18 in (45 cm) in height and in autumn are completely covered with small single flowers in a wide range of colours.

The charms are easily raised from seeds sown in mid-winter and germinated in a temperature of 50°F (10°C). Allow to grow naturally, apart from removing the growing tip when plants are 3-4 in (8-10 cm) high.

Pot initially into 3 in (8 cm) pots, then pot on until plants are in final 8 in (20 cm) pots. Use soil-based potting compost at all stages.

From early spring grow the young plants in a garden frame, then from early summer grow them outdoors. Transfer to the conservatory in early autumn. Water and feed well in summer. Under glass, the plants like airy conditions and a dry atmosphere. Discard after flowering.

Eustoma Poppy-flowered annuals and perennials. The annual *E. grandiflorum* (syn. *Lisianthus russellianus*) has pink, purple, blue or white flowers during summer.

Makes an excellent pot plant. Sow seeds during late winter at 70°F (21°C) and grow in well-drained compost. Water normally during summer. Needs maximum light, including some sun, and airy conditions. Needs long growing season. Can also be sown in autumn.

Lilium (lily) Lilies are ideal bulbs for flowering in pots under glass, after which they should be planted in the garden. There are many suitable kinds such as the yellow and white *L. auratum*; *L. longiflorum*, the Easter lily with pure white blooms; the flamboyant white and pink *L. regale*; and the equally beautiful carmine and pink *L. speciosum* var. *rubrum.*

Bulbs are potted in autumn, setting three per 8 in (20 cm) pot and using soil-based potting compost. Plant shallowly in pots half filled with compost; more compost is added as the stems grow. The pots are best kept in a garden frame over winter and transferred to the conservatory during early or mid-spring. Good ventilation is needed together with steadily moist compost. After flowering return to the frame, keep moist at all times and plant in the garden during autumn.

Oxypetalum The usual species grown is *O. caeruleum* (syn. *Tweedia caerulea*), a herbaceous climber with a twining habit, and clusters of small starry light blue flowers during summer and early autumn. Height 3 ft (1 m).

Grow as an annual in pots, sowing seeds in spring. It likes sunny well-ventilated conditions and well-drained compost. Pinch out shoot tips for a more bushy habit.

Pelargonium, regal Regal pelargoniums make a stunning display in the summer, the flowers coming in shades of red, pink, mauve, purple and white. Plants are best discarded after flowering and replaced with new ones raised from cuttings.

Cuttings can be taken in late summer when they will root without artificial heat. Pot rooted cuttings into 3½ in (9 cm) pots and in early spring move on to 5 in (13 cm) pots. Use soil-based or soilless potting compost.

Regal pelargoniums like sunny conditions (but shade from strong sun), and a dry airy atmosphere. Water as required in summer, but in winter, when conditions are cool, keep the compost only barely moist. Liquid feed flowering plants fortnightly in summer..

Primula Cultivars of *P. obconica*, with red, pink, orange, blue, lilac or white flowers, *P. malacoides* in shades of red, pink, mauve, lilac and white, and the yellow-flowered *P. × kewensis*, herald spring in the cool conservatory.

These primulas are easily raised from seeds and are discarded after flowering. Sow in the spring and germinate in a temperature of 60°F (15.5°C). Prick out seedlings into trays, then move into 3½ in (9 cm) pots, and eventually into final 5 in (13 cm) pots. A soilless compost is recommended.

Primulas should be kept cool, moist (but avoid wetting the leaves), shaded from strong sun and in airy conditions throughout their lives. From early summer to early autumn keep them in a garden frame.

Senecio (cineraria) The heads of daisy-like flowers of the late-winter and spring-flowering cinerarias (*Senecio × hybridus*) come in many colours including red, pink, blue, purple and white.

Plants are easily raised from seeds and are discarded after flowering. Sow between mid-spring and early summer and germinate in a garden frame or other cool place. Otherwise as for primulas, above, avoiding wetting the foliage and taking care not to allow the compost to become very wet.

INTERMEDIATE CONSERVATORY

Permanent plants

Banksia Evergreen shrubs and trees with attractive flowers and/or foliage. The species *B. coccinea* is an attractive shrub about 5 ft (1.5 m) high whose conical bright red flower heads, produced in winter and spring, have conspicuous styles and stigmas.

Grow in pots/tubs of acid well drained soil-based compost, or in a lime-free soil bed. Needs maximum light, sun, and very airy conditions. Moderate watering in growing period, more sparing at other times. Fortnightly liquid feeding during growing period.

Bougainvillea (paper flower) One of the most popular conservatory climbers. Mainly evergreen, the flamboyant summer colour comes from papery bracts that surround the insignificant flowers. Various kinds are grown including *B.* × *buttiana* cultivars 'Mrs Butt' (crimson-magenta), 'Golden Glow' (orange-yellow) and 'Scarlet Queen'; *B.* 'Dania' (deep pink); *B. glabra* (purple); *B.* 'Miss Manilla' (pink); and *B. spectabilis* (red-purple). Height is variable, but in the region of 15 ft (5 m).

Grow in a soil bed, or in large pots/tubs of soil-based compost. Water as required in summer but in winter only as the soil is drying out. Plenty of sunshine required, plus airy conditions and, in summer, humidity. Prune in early spring: if necessary, cut back all stems by one-third; remove any thin or weak shoots completely.

Bromeliads These flamboyant, often colourful and bizarre, relations of the pineapple are ideal conservatory plants, bringing a touch of the tropical rain forest. They are easy to grow, though, and do not need high temperatures. There are lots to choose from, including the air plants or atmospheric tillandsias that are grown on wood, such as a 'plant tree.' Other epiphytes can be grown in the same way, or in pots, including the popular kinds like *Vriesia splendens* (flaming sword), *Aechmea fasciata* (urn plant) and *Nidularium fulgens* (see p.53).

For pot culture, grow in soilless compost, using the smallest possible pots. Keep moist all year round and ensure high humidity when conditions are warm. Air plants are watered by mist spraying daily, or weekly in cool conditions. Ensure good light, but shade from hot sun; and provide airy conditions. Those plants that form their leaves into water-holding vases should have these permanently filled with water, which must be replaced regularly to keep it fresh. Use rain water or soft tap water for bromeliads.

Brunfelsia Evergreen shrubs with a long succession of mainly blue flowers in summer. The species normally grown is

Calliandra haematocephala, a medium-sized evergreen shrub whose pincushion flowers are produced between autumn and spring

B. pauciflora whose blue-purple flowers are fragrant. There are several desirable cultivars, and also worth growing is the wavy white *B. undulata*.

Grow in a soil bed, or in a large pot/tub of soil-based compost. Water when needed in summer, less in winter; liquid feed fortnightly in summer; and provide shade from strong sunshine.

Calliandra Evergreen trees, shrubs and climbers, the species *C. haematocephala* being grown for its pink or white pincushion-like flower heads which consist of many stamens. This autumn to spring flowering shrub reaches 10 ft (3 m) in height.

Grow in large pot or tub of well drained soil-based compost or in a soil bed. Ensure maximum light. Water freely in summer, sparingly in winter, and liquid feed fortnightly during growing season. Stems can be reduced by up to two-thirds to control height.

Chorizema Evergreen shrubs, sub-shrubs and climbers cultivated for flowers. *C. ilicifolium* (holly flame pea) (see p.4) is a small spiny-leaved shrub with colourful orange and pink pea flowers in spring and summer.

Grow in pot or bed of neutral to acid well-drained sandy compost/soil rich in humus. Ensure maximum light, and good ventilation. Water moderately during growing season and sparingly at other times. Feed fortnightly in summer.

Citrus (oranges, lemons) These are superb shrubs or trees for growing in tubs. Even if the temperature is not high enough for fruiting, they make handsome evergreen foliage plants. The flowers are highly fragrant and produced in spring or summer. Typical species available include *C. aurantium* (Seville orange) (see p.56), *C. sinensis* (sweet orange) and *C. limon* (lemon).

Best grown in large pots or tubs of soil-based compost. Water as needed in summer, keep only slightly moist in winter. Liquid feed fortnightly during summer, and when the weather is warm spray the foliage with water. Shade lightly from strong sun and ensure airy conditions. Plants may be stood out of doors for the summer. Maintain shape by shortening shoots by up to two-thirds every two or three years in early spring.

Ferns They are a cool green foil for colourful flowering plants. Plenty are suited to the intermediate conservatory including the very popular *Nephrolepis exaltata* (sword fern) which, incidentally, also looks good in hanging baskets; *Asplenium bulbiferum* (spleenwort); *Pteris tremula* (table fern); and *Adiantum raddianum* (delta maidenhair).

Grow in pots of soilless compost. Ferns should be shaded from direct sun and kept moist throughout the year. When conditions are warm provide humidity and an airy atmosphere. Liquid feed fortnightly during summer.

Hardenbergia Evergreen climbers and sub-shrubs with pea-like flowers. *H. violacea* (syn. *H. monophylla*) (coral pea, Australian sarsparilla) is a 10 ft (3 m) high twining climber with violet, pink or white flowers in spring.

Grow in a pot/tub of soil-based compost, or in a neutral to acid soil bed. Ensure maximum light, water freely in summer, sparingly in winter, and liquid feed fortnightly in summer.

Hibiscus (shrubby mallow) The most popular hibiscus is *H. rosa-sinensis* – or rather its cultivars, with flaring trumpet-shaped flowers in shades of red, pink, yellow, orange and white. It is a deciduous shrub bringing an exotic touch to the conservatory.

Grow in a soil bed, or in a large pot/tub of soil-based compost. Shade lightly from strong sun and provide humidity in warm conditions. Water when necessary in summer but sparingly during winter, liquid feed fortnightly in summer. If desired, prune fairly hard back in late winter.

Impatiens There are several species, but a very striking, unusual, yet easily grown one is *I. niamniamensis*. This bushy evergreen perennial produces masses of helmet-shaped red and yellow flowers in summer and autumn.

Grow in a pot of soilless compost and keep well watered in the growing season, more sparingly at other times. Liquid feed fortnightly in summer and provide humidity. Provide good light, shading from strong sun. Suitable for a shady conservatory.

Pentas Evergreen perennials and shrubs cultivated for flowers. *P. lanceolata* (syn. *P. carnea*) (Egyptian star, star-cluster), is a small shrub with heads of small pink, red, lilac or white star-shaped flowers in summer and autumn.

Grow in a pot/tub of rich, well-drained soil-based compost, or in a soil bed. Maximum light or partial shade are suitable. Water well in summer, sparingly in winter, and liquid feed fortnightly during summer. Can be hard pruned in winter.

Palms Beloved of the Victorians, palms are enjoying renewed popularity. The taller kinds make good focal points, including the feathery *Howeia forsteriana* (thatch-leaf palm) and the prickly, stiff-fronded *Phoenix canariensis* (Canary Island date palm).

Grow in a large pot or tub of soil-based compost. Water as required during summer but in winter only when the soil is drying out. Liquid feed fortnightly in summer. Ensure good light, but shade from strong sunshine.

Tibouchina urvilleana (see p.40) brings a touch of tropical rain forest to intermediate conservatories, flowering in summer and autumn

Plumbago (Cape leadwort) An excellent evergreen climber for the smaller conservatory is *P. auriculata* with beautiful sky-blue flowers in summer and autumn, or white in *P. a.* 'Alba'. Height about 10 ft (3 m).

Grow in a soil bed, or large pot/tub of soil-based compost. Water as needed in summer, but in winter keep only slightly moist. Liquid feed fortnightly in summer. Provide light shade from strong sun. Prune in late winter by reducing side shoots to a few centimetres and cutting back main stems by one-third.

Tibouchina (glory bush) The evergreen shrub *T. urvilleana* (see p.39) produces bowl-shaped blooms of deep violet during the summer and autumn, set against sumptuous velvety foliage. This plant really does create a tropical rain-forest atmosphere.

Grow in a soil bed, or in a large pot/tub of soil-based compost. In summer water as required, but in winter keep the plant only slightly moist. Liquid feed fortnightly in summer. The plant appreciates light shade. Plants can be kept small by cutting them back in winter. It can also be trained on the back wall.

Zantedeschia (arum lily) With its broad arrow-shaped leaves and white arum-like flowers in summer, *Z. aethiopica* is indeed an aristocratic rhizomatous perennial. Even more striking is *Z.* 'Green Goddess' with green, white-splashed spathes.

Plants can be grown in pots of soil-based compost or in a soil bed and should be kept steadily moist all year round. Liquid feed fortnightly in summer. Shade from strong sunshine.

Temporary plants

These plants are discarded when their flower display is over.

Browallia (bush violet) These perennials, which are grown as annual pot plants, produce a profusion of tubular white, blue or lavender flowers in summer.

Sow seeds in early spring and germinate at 65°F (18°C). Can also be sown in late summer for winter flowering. Prick out seedlings into 3 in (8 cm) pots, and pot on as required until plants are in final 5 in (13 cm) pots. Soilless potting compost is recommended. Ensure bright light, but shade from strong sunshine. Water as required. Liquid feed established plants fortnightly in summer.

Celosia (Prince of Wales' feathers) *C. cristata* Plumosa Group has feathery flower heads in summer and autumn, in shades of red, yellow, pink and apricot. They make excellent pot plants and are easily grown from seeds.

Sow early to mid-spring and germinate at 65°F (18°C). Prick out seedlings into 3 in (8 cm) pots and pot on as required until in final

Browallias are temporary pot plants, producing tubular flowers in summer.
Here, *Asparagus densiflorus* 'Sprengeri' makes a pleasing foil

5 in (13 cm) pots. Soilless compost is recommended. Provide bright
light, but shade from strong sunshine. Water as required, avoiding
very wet compost. Liquid feed established plants in summer.

Fuchsia Fuchsia hybrids provide a non-stop display all summer
and into autumn. Depending on habit of growth, they can be
grown as bush plants, as trailers in hanging baskets, or trained to
various forms such as standards, fans and pyramids. (Consult the
Wisley Handbook *Fuchsias* for details of growing and training.)
The trained forms are generally kept for several years, but bush
and basket plants are possibly best renewed each year from
cuttings, discarding the old plants.

To produce bush and basket plants, root soft cuttings in spring
or early summer for flowering plants the following year. Rooting
temperature 65°F (18°C). Start young plants in 3½ in (9 cm) pots
and pot on to final 6-8 in (15-20 cm) pots. Soilless potting compost
is particularly suitable. Pinch out growing tips when plants are
6 in (15 cm) high, and when the resulting lateral shoots are 4 in
(10 cm) long pinch out their tips, too.

Fuchsias should be shaded from strong sun, provided with airy conditions and kept steadily moist. Liquid feed flowering plants fortnightly in summer.

Impatiens (busy lizzie) For their extremely long period of flowering – all summer and into autumn – impatiens have to be regarded as essential conservatory plants. There are various kinds, the seed-raised strains used for bedding making excellent pot plants. Flower colours include shades of red, pink, orange and white. The New Guinea hybrids are particularly attractive as they have bronze foliage.

Seeds are sown in early or mid-spring and germinated in a temperature of 60-65°F (15.6-18.3°C). Impatiens grow well in soilless compost; pot on as necessary. They need copious watering in summer, light shade and high humidity. Liquid feed fortnightly. Discard after flowering.

WARM CONSERVATORY

Permanent plants

Agapetes Attractive flowering shrubs and climbers of which the evergreen climbing *A. macrantha* can be recommended. It has

Agapetes macrantha, an evergreen climber ideally suited to the small conservatory, is particularly valuable as it flowers in winter

Anthurium scherzerianum, left, is an evergreen perennial whose brilliantly coloured spathes will light up a shady part of the conservatory. The distinctive inflorescences of *Aphelandra squarrosa* 'Louisae', right (see p.44), appear in summer and autumn – for the rest of the year enjoy the foliage

pendulous urn-shaped pink or white red-patterned flowers in winter. Height up to 6 ft (1.8 m).

Grow in a pot, tub or bed of humus rich, moisture retentive yet well-drained acid to neutral soil/compost. Succeeds in maximum light or partial shade. Water freely in summer, at which time liquid feed fortnightly, and moderately during winter.

Aglaonema (Chinese evergreen) These low evergreen clump-forming perennials are grown for their handsome broad lance-shaped foliage. There are numerous species, but cultivars of *A. commutatum* are widely grown, the leaves being marked with white or silver.

Grow in beds or pots. Excellent results are obtained in soilless compost. Provide warm humid conditions and a spot out of direct sun for these shade-loving plants. Water as needed in summer, keeping on the dry side in winter. Liquid feed fortnightly in summer.

Anthurium These evergreen perennials create an exotic touch with their colourful spathes: bright scarlet in the species *A. scherzerianum* and scarlet or orange-red in *A. andreanum.* In recent years other colours have appeared such as shades of pink, orange and white.

Provide warm, humid conditions and shade. Grow in pots of soilless compost, watering as needed in summer, but in winter keeping it only slightly moist. Liquid feed fortnightly in summer.

Aphelandra (zebra plant) The perennial *A. squarrosa* 'Louisae' (see p.43) has large leaves with conspicuous white veins, and pyramid-shaped inflorescences in summer and autumn consisting of bright yellow bracts and small yellow flowers.

Generally grown in pots of soilless or soil-based compost. In warm conditions provide humidity; shade from strong sun; maintain the compost steadily moist; and liquid feed fortnightly in summer. To prevent tall bare stems, cut the plant back by about one-third to half after flowering.

Begonia This is a huge genus, the members of which are ideally suited to the warm conservatory, both flowering and foliage species and hybrids. Of the former there are many attractive kinds like the winter-flowering *B.* × *cheimantha* 'Gloire de Lorraine' and cultivars of *B. hiemalis.* The cane-stemmed begonias, like *B.* × *corallina* which has silver-spotted foliage and pink flowers, can also be recommended. For foliage there are begonias like *B.* × *erythrophylla* whose leaves have striking red undersides; *B. serratipetala* with serrated bronzy foliage; and *B. metallica* with bronze-green leaves, red on the underside.

Grow in pots, using soilless compost. Do not allow very wet conditions: ensure compost partially dries out between waterings. Humidity is essential in warm conditions; shade from strong sun but ensure bright light. Liquid feed fortnightly.

Codiaeum (croton) These flamboyant multicoloured evergreen foliage shrubs provide a lush tropical effect to the warm conservatory. Leaf shape, size and colour are variable.

Grow in beds or pots, ideally using soil-based compost in the latter. Pinch out growing tips of young plants to ensure bushy specimens. High temperatures and humidity will ensure lush growth, together with good light, but shade from strong sunshine. Water as needed in summer but cut down in winter. Liquid feed fortnightly in summer.

Cordyline For the warm conservatory the cultivars of *C. fruticosa* (syn. *C. terminalis*) (Ti tree) are recommended. This shrub is evergreen with bold sword-shaped leaves and it can grow quite tall, although slow, eventually making a good specimen plant. There are cultivars with red and green leaves.

Grow in beds or pots, in the latter using soil-based compost. Warmth and humidity are needed together with light shade from the sun. In summer water as required, but in winter water sparingly. Liquid feed fortnightly in summer.

Crotalaria Attractive pea-flowered evergreen shrubs, perennials and annuals. *C. agatiflora* (canary-bird bush) is a 10 ft (3 m) high evergreen shrub with green-yellow flowers in summer and at other times.

Grow in a pot/tub of well drained soil-based compost or in a soil bed. Needs maximum light. Water freely in summer, moderately during winter and liquid feed fortnightly in summer. Reduce old stems by half after flowering.

Ficus The classic conservatory species is *F. benjamina*, the weeping fig, which makes a fine specimen plant when it has attained some height. This small evergreen tree has small leaves, in shape like those of the related rubber plant, rich green and shiny. It has a pendulous habit of growth, unusual among conservatory plants.

Grow in a large pot or tub, using soil-based potting compost. Warm conditions with humidity are needed, together with bright light, but shade from strong sunshine. Water as required in summer, but in winter allow compost to partially dry out between waterings. Liquid feed fortnightly in summer.

Gardenia (Cape jasmine) The evergreen shrub *G. jasminoides* has the most exquisitely fragrant white flowers in the summer and autumn.

Grow in a bed for maximum size (about 6 ft [1.8 m] high), or in a large pot or tub of soil-based potting compost. Growth is also good in soilless compost but it may not be able to support a large plant adequately. Acid to neutral soil is required. Plenty of humidity is needed when temperatures are high, and partial shade. Water as required in summer, but reduce in winter. Liquid feed fortnightly in summer. Young plants should have their growing tips pinched out to induce a bushy habit. After flowering prune back stems by about half their length.

Hymenocallis Bulbs, some evergreen, with daffodil-like scented flowers. *H. × macrostephana* is evergreen and produces large white or cream flowers in spring or summer.

Grow in a pot of well drained soil-based compost. Water normally, but reduce considerably in winter – however, avoid drying out. Plants prefer a good level of humidity and light shade from hot sun. Liquid feed in summer. Repot in spring.

Mandevilla These flamboyant evergreen or deciduous climbers produce trumpet-shaped flowers in the spring or summer. The most common species is *Mandevilla splendens* (syn. *Dipladenia splendens*) which provides a long succession of rose-pink flowers during late spring and early summer. It will attain a height of at least 10 ft (3 m).

Grow in a bed or large pot/tub, using well drained soil-based potting compost in the container. High humidity is appreciated in summer together with light shade from strong sun. Water as needed in summer, but in winter only when soil is drying out. If size needs to be contained, prune the plant back hard when flowering is over, cutting the previous season's stems back to within 2 in (5 cm) of their base. Alternatively, if you want a larger plant, leave it unpruned, except for thinning out congested growth as necessary.

Medinilla The spectacular *M. magnifica* is an evergreen shrub about 5 ft (1.5 m) high with deeply veined leaves and pendulous trusses of pink flowers below large pink bracts during spring and summer. Grow in a pot of humus-rich compost, such as a soilless type. Provide partial shade and high humidity; water well in summer, when fortnightly liquid feeding can be carried out, and moderately during winter.

Philodendron For creating a lush jungle-like effect in a warm conservatory, there are few plants to surpass the philodendrons, which are grown for their bold foliage. They are evergreen shrubs and climbers, the latter producing aerial roots on their stems. There are lots to choose from, including the climbers *P. angustisectum* (syn. *P. elegans*) with deeply cut foliage; *P.* 'Burgundy' whose leaves are flushed with red and are wine-red on the undersides; the copper-flushed *P. erubescens*; *P. pedatum* whose glossy oval leaves are dark green; and *P. tuxtlanum* 'Tuxtla' which has glossy foliage. Non-climbing philodendrons include the large-growing *P. pinnatifidum* with wide-spreading deeply cut leaves.

Grow in soil beds or large pots/tubs. Philodendrons like humus-rich soil. A good compost consists of equal parts, by volume, of soil-based and soilless potting compost. Climbing philodendrons are best grown up a moss pole; alternatively train against the back wall of the conservatory. Main requirements are warmth, high humidity and shade from strong sunshine. Water as required in summer, but during winter allow the soil to partially dry out between waterings. Liquid feed fortnightly during summer.

Pycnostachys Attractive bushy perennials with whorls of tubular flowers. *P. dawei* has beautiful bright blue flowers in winter and spring and red-backed foliage. Height up to 5 ft (1.5 m).

Grow in a pot of rich well drained soil-based compost or in a soil bed. Provide maximum light. Water freely in summer, sparingly during winter. Liquid feed fortnightly during growing season.

Pyrostegia The evergreen tendril climber *P. venusta* (flame vine or flower, golden shower) has spectacular golden-orange tubular

Medinilla magnifica, one of the aristocrats of the conservatory, is an evergreen shrub with distinctive foliage and flowers

flowers in clusters from autumn to spring. It quickly attains 30 ft (10 m).

Grow in a large pot/tub of rich well drained soil-based compost or, even better, in a soil bed. Ensure maximum light, humidity, water freely in very warm conditions, but reduce in lower temperatures. Liquid feed fortnightly in summer. If congested, thin out older stems after flowering.

Sanchezia Evergreen shrubs, climbers and perennials, attractive flowering and foliage plants. The 5 ft (1.5 m) tall shrub *S. speciosa*

Conservatory plants need caring for properly and on a regular basis if they are to grow well. This means:

- Pot and feed when required.
- Pay attention to watering.
- Provide the right atmosphere and other growing conditions.
- Prune, if required.
- Control pests and diseases.

COMPOSTS AND POTTING

In the descriptive lists suitable types of potting compost have been recommended. For most permanent plants soil-based compost is recommended: John Innes potting compost. JIP1 is used for initial potting of young plants, JIP2 for potting on, and JIP3 when planting in large pots or tubs.

Soilless composts are recommended for some plants, especially temporary pot plants and permanent kinds that like humus-rich soil, and these imply peat-based or the new peatless composts.

Plastic pots are widely used for growing conservatory plants (especially temporary pot plants), but for larger specimens I recommend the heavier clay pots as they are more stable. Plants should be potted on as required, generally before they become pot-bound (pots packed full of roots). Plants are often moved on two sizes – for example, from a 4 in (10 cm) to a 6 in (15 cm) pot – although very slow-growing plants should be moved on one size each time.

Eventually many permanent plants, like shrubs, trees and perennials, will need to go into final containers. These may be large pots, maybe ornamental kinds, or wooden tubs, the square Versailles design being particularly attractive in conservatories. Final containers will vary in size but should be a minimum of 12 in (30 cm) in diameter and depth, through to 18 in (45 cm) or more, depending on size of plant.

Plenty of headroom is needed for the vigorous climber *Solandra maxima*, above (see p.48), whose huge scented flowers are produced during spring and summer. *Tecoma stans*, below (see p.48), is a large shrub with attractive ferny foliage and produces trumpet-shaped flowers between spring and autumn

Permanent plants are best potted on annually in early spring. Temporary pot plants may need moving on throughout the growing season as well.

Drainage material is often dispensed with these days but I feel it is necessary when using pots over 6 in (15 cm) in diameter and certainly for final containers. 'Crocks' or broken clay pots still provide the best drainage material and the layer should be covered with rough leafmould or something similar before adding compost. Make sure you leave watering space at the top of the pot or container – from ½ in (12 mm) to 1 in (2.5 cm) according to size.

Repotting

Plants in final containers will need to have some of their compost replaced every couple of years or so as it starts to deteriorate. This involves repotting into the same container in early spring.

Remove the plant from the container and reduce the size of the root ball by at least 2 in (5 cm) all round by teasing away compost and root pruning if necessary. Then replace in the same container – which should have been cleaned out and be perfectly dry – and work fresh compost all around the root ball, right down to the bottom.

In the interim years simply top dress with fresh compost after removing the top 1 in (2.5 cm) or so.

PLANTING

Planting in raised beds is the same as planting container-grown plants outdoors. Simply make a hole slightly larger than the root ball, remove the plant from its pot carefully to avoid root disturbance, place it in the centre of the hole, work fine soil around it and firm well. The top of the root ball should be covered with about ½ in (12 mm) of soil. With container-grown plants planting can be carried out at any time of year.

Finish off by mulching the surface of the soil about 2 in (5 cm) deep with pulverised bark or coconut fibre.

PLUNGING

This attractive method of displaying plants in pots ensures a humid atmosphere around them. Plunging is recommended for displaying groups of plants in planters (large deep floor containers), or single plants in ornamental pot holders.

Nidularium fulgens (see p.36) is one of the more flamboyant bromeliads, bringing a touch of the tropical rain forest to the intermediate conservatory

The pots are plunged up to their rims in water-absorbing horticultural aggregate, peat or coconut fibre, which is then kept constantly moist to provide atmospheric humidity.

WATERING

Specific watering needs have been given for the plants in the descriptive lists. Plants do vary in their water requirements, some having to be kept steadily moist all year round, others relishing plenty of water in the growing period (spring and summer), but far less in autumn and winter when they are resting.

There are various ways of determining when water is required. The usual technique is to push a finger down into the compost. If during the growing period it is dry on top and moist below, then water is needed. However, if moist or wet on the surface do not water. If during the resting period (when we may need to water more sparingly, keeping the compost only slightly moist), the compost surface is dry and it feels dryish lower down, water can be applied. Then leave alone until the compost is drying out again.

When watering always completely fill the space between the rim of the pot and the surface of the compost to ensure the entire depth of compost is moistened.

Test soil beds in the same way, but this time apply enough water to penetrate to a depth of at least 6 in (15 cm): approximately nearly 5 gallons per square yard (27 litres per square metre).

Soil or compost may also be tested for water requirements with the aid of a soil-moisture meter.

Some conservatory plants prefer soft (lime-free) water, especially lime-hating plants (those that need acid compost or soil) and bromeliads. Rainwater is ideal for these.

HUMIDITY

Many conservatory plants relish a humid or moist atmosphere in warm conditions – say from 60°F (15.5°C) upwards – and some need very high humidity, particularly many of the tropical foliage plants. This is indicated in the descriptive lists. Some plants, however, need dry air all year round, including desert cacti and succulents and pelargoniums.

Humidity should not be provided in cool conditions – once the temperature drops below about 50°F (10°C) – as then the air must be kept as dry as possible.

In the lived-in conservatory humidity has to be provided locally around the plants – no one wants to live in rain-forest conditions, and it would do the furnishings no good at all. Local humidity can be provided by plunging plants (see p.52) or by mist spraying the leaves several times a day with soft tap water or rain water. Do not mist spray hairy or woolly plants, though. In a conservatory devoted purely to plants, one can damp down the floor and staging twice a day, morning and evening.

On staging, gravel trays filled with horticultural aggregate will provide local humidity if the aggregate is kept moist.

VENTILATION

Ventilation is needed all year round to maintain fresh healthy conditions in the conservatory. It can also be used to help reduce temperature and humidity. Ventilation should always be consistent with maintaining the temperature required.

Effective ventilation is provided by opening roof ventilators and side windows or vents. Then the warm air rises and escapes through the conservatory roof and draws in cool air from lower levels.

SHADING

During the spring and summer shading will be needed by plants and people. Hot sun shining through the glass can scorch plants badly. Shading will also help to keep the temperature down and can be used in conjunction with ventilation.

Ideally provide shade only when the sun is shining, removing it at other times to ensure plants receive maximum light.

There are some groups of plants, though, that do not need shading. These include the desert cacti and succulents, perhaps not the ideal choice for the conservatory that is also used as a living room and contains plants that need shade.

Do not use shading in autumn and winter, as then plants need maximum light. While on this subject, do remember to keep the glass scrupulously clean to ensure optimum light transmission. This, again, is especially important in autumn and winter.

FEEDING PLANTS

Conservatory plants need feeding between mid-spring and early autumn (the growing period), never between mid-autumn and early spring when they may be resting or growth has slowed down. Never feed newly potted or repotted plants as the fresh compost will keep them going until new roots have permeated it – about eight weeks on average. Never feed plants if the soil or compost is dry – moisten it first.

During the growing period fortnightly liquid feeding is ideal for most potted plants, using a houseplant fertilizer based on seaweed. There are fertilizers formulated for foliage and flowering plants.

To cut down on frequency of feeding, consider using fertilizer tablets for potted plants, these being pushed into the compost where they slowly release their nutrients over several weeks.

Plants in soil beds can be fed by lightly forking a dry general-purpose fertilizer into the soil surface in mid-spring. This can be followed by monthly liquid feeds during summer if you feel plant growth needs a boost.

PRUNING

In the descriptive lists specific details of pruning have been given where required. Here we will look at the general principles.

Use a pair of very sharp secateurs for pruning to ensure really clean, smooth cuts which heal quickly.

Pruning cuts should always be made just above growth buds, which are situated in the axils between leaf stalks and stems. Never leave a portion of stem above a bud, or this will die back, and do not make the cut so near the bud that it is damaged.

Any large pruning cuts on shrubs – 1 in (2.5 cm) or more in

Citrus aurantium, the Seville orange (see p.38). Even if the temperature is not high enough for fruiting, citrus make handsome evergreen foliage plants

diameter – should be treated with a proprietary pruning compound to prevent diseases from entering.

Not all plants require regular pruning by any means, but occasional attention may be required. Cut back any dead and dying growth to live wood as required. Dead flowers should be removed to maintain a tidy appearance and prevent infection from botrytis.

PESTS AND DISEASES

Aphids
Greenfly are the most common aphids found under glass. They feed in colonies on tender shoot tips and leaves, sucking the sap which weakens the plant and distorts growth. Spray with pirimicarb, pyrethrum or an insecticidal soap as soon as noticed.

Botrytis (grey mould)
This is the most common fungal disease, attacking a wide range of plants, causing parts to rot. It takes the form of a grey mould on

flowers, leaves and stems and in the right conditions can spread rapidly. To prevent it, avoid very damp conditions and provide plenty of ventilation. Control botrytis by spraying plants with a benomyl, carbendazim or thiophanate-methyl fungicide (ideally taking them outdoors). Also cut off affected parts of plants.

Glasshouse red spider mite
Microscopic yellowish-green or reddish spider-like creatures, which feed on leaves resulting in fine pale mottling, can be deterred by mist spraying leaves daily with plain water. Spray with malathion, pirimiphos-methyl or an insecticidal soap as soon as noticed. Alternatively try biological control, using the predatory mite *Phytoseiulus persimilis* (do not use pesticides where biological controls have been introduced).

Mealybug
These soft grey-white plant bugs with a white woolly covering feed on the stems of many plants, especially woody kinds. Dab pests with an artist's brush dipped in methylated spirits, or spray plants with malathion or pirimiphos-methyl. Biological control with a ladybird, *Cryptolaemus montrouzieri*, can reduce infestations during the summer.

Mildew, powdery
A fungal disease appearing as a white powdery deposit on leaves and shoot tips of many plants, often causes distorted growth. Spray affected plants with a benomyl, bupirimate with triforine, carbendazim, fenarimol (with permethrin), propiconazole, sulphur or thiophanate-methyl fungicide (ideally taking them outdoors).

Scale insects
These generally brownish insects, resembling shells and immobile, feed on stems and leaves of many plants, especially woody kinds. Spray plants with malathion or pirimiphos-methyl.

Whitefly
Tiny white winged insects with flat oval scale-like nymphs congregate in colonies on the undersides of leaves of many conservatory plants, where they suck the sap. As soon as noticed, spray with permethrin, pyrethrum or an insecticidal soap. Alternatively try biological control, using the parasitic wasp *Encarsia formosa*. Do not use pesticides where biological control has been introduced.

Effective Displays

Owning a conservatory provides an excellent opportunity of creating some imaginative plant displays. Somehow, potted plants simply stood on the staging without much thought do not look right in the relatively grand surroundings of a conservatory – a much better effect is achieved if they are grouped together, and especially if they contrast in colour, shape and texture. Remember that all plants in a group should require the same conditions such as temperature and light.

It has already been mentioned in the chapter on Fixtures and Fittings that tiered staging allows one to create impressive and professional-looking plant displays, especially with the liberal use of trailing plants. But using staging is not the only way of displaying potted plants. Groups can be created on the floor, too, such as matching ones either side of the conservatory or interior door, or semi-circular groups in the corners.

The following ideas show how some of the plants in the descriptive lists can be used effectively, plus a few extras for adding the finishing touches.

SEASONAL GROUPS

In the conservatories and greenhouses of many private and public gardens you will find that seasonal plant groups are popular. Why not reflect the different seasons in your conservatory with appropriate pot plants? Here is a taster of the countless possibilities.

Cool conservatory
The cool conservatory in spring could feature camellias. Surround these with pots of spring bulbs like narcissus and hyacinths, and pots of the greenhouse primulas *P. malacoides* or *P. obconica*.

For summer colour try bold groups of regal pelargoniums, with a foil of *Chlorophytum comosum* 'Variegatum', the ubiquitous but

A spring group which features daffodils, silver-leaved cyclamen and primulas – an ideal plant association in a cool conservatory useful spider plant with green and white striped grassy foliage.

Autumn could bring bold groups of charm chrysanthemums, which do not really need any other plants with them.

Intermediate conservatory
Bush fuchsias, with standards to give height, make impressive groups for summer-long colour. Foliage plants create an excellent foil, such as the variegated abutilons *A.* × *hybridum* 'Savitzii' and *A. striatum* 'Thompsonii'.

Celosia cristata Plumosa Group is a favourite display plant, its brilliant feathery flower heads produced over a long period in summer and autumn contrasting beautifully with 'cool' ferns such as *Pteris tremula* and *Asplenium bulbiferum*.

Strelitzia reginae (see p.33), an evergreen perennial, takes five to seven years to reach flowering size – but it is worth the wait, and it has good foliage

PERMANENT GROUPS

Try to group permanent plants together as attractively as possible, using flowering and foliage kinds. This is quite easily achieved whether plants are in pots or soil beds. For instance, in the **cool** conservatory a group consisting of *Clivia miniata*, *Lantana camara* and *Strelitzia reginae* offers plenty of contrast, especially in shape.

In the **intermediate** conservatory, foliage plants like ferns, together with zantedeschia or arum lily, can be grouped around such plants as brunfelsia and hibiscus to create attractive groups.

In the **warm** conservatory, one can create some really colourful and flamboyant groups with tropical flowering and foliage plants. Creating single-colour groups can be fun, such as a red group using, for example, anthuriums with red spathes, codiaeums with a predominance of red in their leaves, red-leaved cordylines and perhaps the red-flushed *Philodendron* 'Burgundy'. Here there will also be dramatic contrast in leaf shape.

CREATING HEIGHT

For some inexplicable reason, home gardeners often fail to achieve adequate height in groups of plants, arranging them all on one level thereby creating flat-looking displays. Professional gardeners invariably elevate some of the plants in groups to create height. For instance, in floor displays that are viewed all round, the plants in the centre could be tall, or elevated, gradually grading to shorter material towards the edges. This could create, for instance, a pyramid or cone shape.

When arranging plants on ordinary bench-type staging, place tall (or elevated) specimens at the back and again gradually grade down to the front with shorter plants.

How does one create height? Either use taller plants, or elevate plants on upturned flower pots. Also, one can use climbers to create height in groups, such as philodendrons on moss poles in the warm conservatory.

If one needs to hide pots, such as those used to elevate plants, then fill in with pots of trailing foliage plants such as small-leaved hardy ivies (cultivars of *Hedera helix*) which are very adaptable and can be used in any temperature, or *Asparagus densiflorus* 'Sprengeri' (a favourite of the professionals and suited to the intermediate or warm conservatory).

A useful trick to help in hiding pots, and so on, is to slightly tilt the pots of trailers forwards. They can be supported with little blocks of wood, or something similar. Obviously they have to be stood upright for watering, but it is often worth the effort to achieve a professional-looking display.

TRAILING PLANTS

Apart from their obvious role in elevated containers, trailing plants are very useful for including around or along the edge of groups, particularly those arranged on staging. They can be used to hide edges of staging and pots. Ivies and asparagus have already been mentioned; others to consider are: *Epipremnum aureum* cultivars with marbled foliage, warm conservatory; *Ficus pumila*, the creeping fig, with green leaves, intermediate or warm; *Oplismenus hirtellus* 'Variegatus', green and white striped grass, intermediate or warm; and *Stenotaphrum secundatum* 'Variegatum', a cream and green striped grass, intermediate or warm.

SPECIMEN PLANTS

Large specimen plants are very much in vogue for interior landscaping and particularly popular are tall bare-stemmed plants with a tuft of leaves at the top, such as large yuccas and dracaenas. Large specimens create a sense of maturity in a conservatory and make impressive focal points when positioned in corners or each side of doors. Palms are enjoying renewed popularity (they were in vogue during the Victorian period). It is possible to buy large specimens of numerous species, including those mentioned in the descriptive lists – *Howeia forsteriana* (thatch-leaf palm) and *Phoenix canariensis* (Canary Island date palm), both for the intermediate conservatory.

In warm conditions *Cordyline fruticosa* cultivars (Ti tree) and the ubiquitous *Ficus benjamina* (weeping fig) make excellent specimen plants. One could also use climbing philodendrons trained to moss poles. Although not included in the lists, *Yucca elephantipes* deserves a mention here. It develops a thick trunk supporting at the top a rosette of green, erect sword-like leaves, and is suitable for the intermediate or warm conservatory.

This display of tropical foliage plants in a warm conservatory has been elevated by means of tiered wooden staging

Index

Page numbers in italic type indicate illustrations

LE HAMMAM

d'Othman Khadraoui

LE HAMMAM

d'Othman Khadraoui

Conçu et présenté par :
Lizbeth Pelinq et Anne Thuaudet

Bas-reliefs en bois polyvhromes

Textes de

Hédi Turki - Férid Boughedir - Samir Ayadi - Zohra Jlassi
Abdelaziz Kacem - Rafik El Kamel - Emna Bel Hadj Yahia
Mahmoud Sehili - Aroussia Nallouti - Hamida Ben Ammar
Nefla Dhab - Mohamed Driss - Sophie El Goulli - Ali Bellagha
Moncef Dhouib - Anouar Brahem - Ali Louati - Fadhila Chebbi
Lotfi Ben Abderrazak - Traki Bouchrara Zannad
Rachid Koraïchi - Alia Tabaï
Abdel Wahad Bouhdiba

Cérès Productions

ISBN 9973 - 19 - 000 - 9

© 1992 - Cérès Productions
6, Avenue Abderrahman Azzam - 1002 Tunis
Fax : 787.516

Avant-propos

Ce livre est l'histoire d'un coup de cœur.

L'idée originale en revient à Wanda de Bosschère qui, la première, a découvert Othman Khadraoui et ses tableaux de bois de palmier. Touchées par sa sensibilité et sa naïveté d'expression, nous avons voulu que cet ouvrage collectif lui soit un hommage.

Autour d'Othman s'est constituée une chaîne de complicités amicales: rencontres privilégiées avec nos auteurs, dans l'admiration commune d'un art primitif et magique.

Moments délicieux que ceux de la découverte de l'autre... chaque manuscrit donné en mains propres était comme un secret livré d'abord à nous, puis à vous lecteurs.
Tandis que nos doigts caressaient les sculptures que l'artiste tirait de son grand sac de jute, les mots-poèmes reçus prenaient tout leur sens.

Parler du hammam c'est pousser une porte et entrer dans l'intimité des êtres, dans le monde du souvenir, des émotions et des sensations.

Les mains d'Othman ont façonné pièce après pièce la représentation d'un univers clos. Les auteurs nous enseignent dans le merveilleux kaléidoscope de leurs visions particulières la richesse et la diversité de la vie.

Inséparables sont l'Art et le simple art de vivre.

Lizbeth Pelinq   *Anne Thuaudet*

Hammam

L'art naïf, l'imagerie populaire, l'expression enfantine sont souvent à l'honneur. Othman KHADRAOUI, un grand enfant pas très jeune et un artiste original, propose des œuvres difficiles à oublier, faciles à placer. Il se veut, à la fois, sculpteur et peintre. Utilisant des morceaux de planches de bois récupérés ça et là, il les sculpte sur une face en une sorte de bas-relief et ensuite, il peint les creux et les saillies. L'effet baigne dans l'innocence, la joie et la lumière. L'enfant adulte s'amuse, il est heureux et il nous communique son bonheur, sinon sa bonne humeur.

Aussi, le sujet du bain maure ou hammam a été souvent traité par cet artiste qui n'a pas manqué, chaque fois, de le développer avec une verve étonnante, exprimant si bien le caractère et la couleur du pays.

Hédi Turki
Peintre

8

Biographie d'Othman Khadraoui

Né le 1er Février 1938 à Sidi Bouzid. A l'âge de 20 ans, il apprend à lire et à écrire grâce à un programme d'alphabétisation.

Père de 7 enfants, il habite dans un quartier populaire de Tunis. De ses sculptures ayant pour thème le hammam il déclare : «le hammam est le lien entre la croyance et la propreté».

Hammam

A chacun son hammam...

Hammam pudique et secret. Hammam troublant et équivoque. Hammam mystérieux et fantastique. Hammam des corps indécis remodelés par la buée... Hammam espace sonore démultiplié par l'écho à l'infini. Hammam de toutes les frayeurs, de tous les rêves. Hammam du dévoilement et de la honte vive et passagère. Hammam des formes lumineuses de gouttes d'eau ou de sueur. Hammam ventre maternel, refuge, sombre, chaud et liquide, où l'on vous prend en charge, où l'on s'abandonne avec langueur. Hammam où l'on vous bouscule, vous masse, vous peigne, vous houspille. Hammam où tout est lisse et tout glisse... hors de l'univers réel. Hammam espace de jeux, espace de détente, de bavardages, de rires et de cris, d'oubli et d'épluchures d'oranges... Hammam de la caresse lourde du *tfal* et de l'odeur prenante du géranium.
J'ai essayé de dire le mien, celui de mon enfance, par l'image et le son dans le film Halfaouine *"Asfour Stah"*...
En voici aujourd'hui quelques autres, dits par la peinture et le texte, avec des talents forts et multiples.
Car le hammam est Un et multiple.
Il y a tant de hammams...

Ferid Boughedir
Cinéaste

Hammam

Du Kouttâb... au Hammam !

 Dès qu'il avait essuyé sa planche inondée d'argile, l'enfant descendait l'escalier du *kouttâb*, se faufilait entre les passants et les charretiers qui se bousculaient dans la rue étroite, et courait vers l'entrée du Hammam pour y goûter la fraîcheur d'un parfum de souvenir. Assis sur une *doukkana*, à même le carrelage craquelé, il passait le temps à regarder des femmes qui, sans se soucier de sa présence, entraient et sortaient dans l'anonymat de leur *sefsâri*. De toutes les façons, il n'était pas arrivé à l'âge où la *hârza* devait l'exclure du monde merveilleux des corps qui, comme sa planche, se barbouillaient d'argile pour couvrir les signes d'une induration inexorable. Mais comme sa mère ne devait l'y introduire qu'une fois par semaine...

Jamais il n'avait fait de rapprochement entre le Kouttâb où il apprenait des mots sans en saisir le sens, et le Hammam où il était saisi de sensations sans en dire un mot. Pourtant il savait que les deux établissements avaient des portes d'entrée sur la rue parfaitement identiques : deux volets en bois massif qui formaient un demi-cercle en haut et un carré parfait à la base, tous deux enduits d'un vert tendre où le rouge parfaitement centré et cerné de blanc devait rappeler la géométrie de l'ensemble. Il en était de même pour les deux faux piliers qui en assuraient la garde dans une spirale des deux couleurs complémentaires toujours séparées par la blancheur d'un filet indiscernable. «Mais - comme lui disait sa mère - c'est la porte du Hammam qui est la plus grande». Alors, pour une raison qu'il ne devinait pas assez, il en était ravi...

12

Hélas ! comme il ne pouvait y passer toute son après-midi, il commençait, le soir tombant, à chercher des yeux une voisine qui, le reconnaissant, lui tirerait l'oreille droite ou gauche, en le grondant sévèrement sur le chemin de la maison. «Qu'importe ! se disait-il, pourvu qu'elle ne me lâche pas avant l'arrivée, et que je puisse sentir encore cette fraîcheur d'argile ambrée qui se dégage de son aisselle et embaume tout le quartier jusqu'à... demain».

Aujourd'hui encore, par nostalgie ou par curiosité, il lui plaît de revenir à ce vieux faubourg de Tunis pour essayer de comprendre les raisons du choix de ce rouge et de ce vert qui ne s'épousent guère.

Même si dans la nouvelle configuration de la ville, un architecte sans scrupules, a cru devoir tout détruire jusqu'à la moindre fraîcheur d'âme, dans la mémoire de l'enfant, devenu adulte, résonne une question comme une chanson lancinante :

«Et si ce filet blanc était là justement pour empêcher que le feu de la Géhenne n'embrasât les vergers du paradis ?»

«Allez donc savoir !» se dit-il toujours avant d'éteindre la lumière et de fermer à nouveau les yeux.

Samir Ayadi
Ecrivain

Hammam

«Mariage de jouissance» au hammam !

Une gamine fluette s'élance de ma mémoire et ramasse avec une joie enfantine le nécessaire pour le hammam. Elle oint d'huile d'olive ses nattes blondes...

Voisines et proches déjà regroupées, le cortège se met en route. Les femmes adorent le hammam. Elles déambulent lentement alourdies de leurs futures parures.

Quand leurs pas foulent le sol de cet espace aquatique féminin, elles se conforment aux rites du hammam : la gardienne est à l'affût des négligentes et des contrevenantes.

Au centre du vacarme du hammam se dessine la géographie des corps avec leurs reliefs et leurs dépressions.

Chaque baigneuse s'adonne toute entière au rite de son bain qui débute dans la pièce «chaude», là où s'ouvre un œil audacieux dévorant les corps alanguis; l'œil du bassin chaud guette les baigneuses, attentif à leurs méditations. Le vacarme s'assourdit car rares sont celles qui se blottissent dans cet espace.

Ici la vapeur parcourt le corps, les cœurs s'ouvrent, tristesse et joie se mettent à nu, tombent les secrets.

Lorsque la chaleur devient trop intense, les baigneuses quittent cet espace aux cris de *quattous ! quattous !*. Les corps s'allègent et se transforment en spectres enivrés au milieu de ce dancing vaporeux.

Après l'enlacement de la vapeur la baigneuse s'absorbe dans ce corps qu'elle célèbre, le frictionnant énergiquement pour se consacrer ensuite à la caresse du *tfal*. Elle en enduit méticuleusement son corps tout entier, le masse soigneusement comme si elle souhaitait le recréer ou le remodeler dans son inconscient en commençant par les mèches de cheveux, jusqu'à la plante des pieds.

Chacune résiste au temps, aux souffrances, aux tristesses et aux rides dans le mouvement recommencé du massage. L'argile s'estompe pour que resplendisse la pureté et que triomphe le jet d'eau chaude. A la mesure de sa violence, grandit la griserie des corps. L'eau se transforme en créature douée d'un corps, d'une âme, d'une voix, elle glisse sur les corps assoiffés, s'y insinue, pénètre au plus profond des lieux intimes, s'y unit.

Les corps éclatent, beaux, splendides. Ils vivent un mariage de jouissance avec l'eau, rejetant de côté toutes les limites et les interdits. c'est la noce licite dans les us et coutumes du hammam. Et dans l'espace de l'isoloir, les corps épanouis se livrent à la virilité de l'eau. Le corps entrave se transforme en corps espace.

Zohra Jlassi
Ecrivain

---

* Traduit par Jean Fontaine

Hammam

H ypnose à la vapeur qu'un demi-jour déroute

A bandon à la main qu'on espère et redoute

M arbre amolli le corps frémit par tous les pores

M urée l'âme s'endort et l'esprit s'évapore

A h l'extase ambiguë la sensuelle ascèse

M imique où l'on rejoue l'initiale genèse

[signature]

Abdelaziz Kacem
Ecrivain - poète

Hammam

 Dans ma mémoire d'enfant, aller avec ma mère au hammam était jour de grande toilette : source de plaisir mêlé de crainte et même de frayeur à l'idée de la sensation d'étouffement qui m'envahirait dans la pièce la plus chaude.

Devenu grand, j'accompagnais mon père. C'était la fête car je savais qu'après, nous irions déjeuner dehors d'une succulente soupe de *lablabi* qui nous était refusée à la maison.

Nous partions très tôt le matin, parfois dans la nuit, ce qui ajoutait un pincement au cœur.

Imaginez... vous entrez... il n'y a personne. Vous vous dirigez vers la pièce la plus chaude pour y transpirer, les pieds dans l'eau bouillante. Quand c'est votre tour, le *tayeb* aux mains de fée vous appelle et là, c'est extraordinaire. Cette impression que non seulement il vous décrasse mais qu'il vous offre en plus une peau neuve, l'ancienne restant là, à côté de vous, en petits tas.

Le hammam, c'est vaste, c'est grand, ça vous écrase par son ampleur. Vous marchez dedans et c'est comme si vous marchiez hors du temps. Vous croisez des centenaires, des gens sans âge, immobiles et aveugles.

Le temps n'a pas de prise sur ce lieu. Depuis des siècles, les hommes sont dans la même tenue... la *fouta* est la même...

On laisse sa vie au vestiaire. On ne se concentre que sur soi-même, on regarde sans voir.

Et puis... être entouré de gens propres vous réconcilie avec le monde. C'est le pouvoir fabuleux du hammam.

Rafik El Kamel
Peintre

Hammam

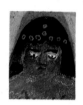

Je me souviens encore de l'humidité ambiante du hammam, de cette vapeur qui mettait des nuages dans ma tête, des larmes dans mes yeux, des odeurs fortes de *tfal* et de *henné* dans mes narines. Je me souviens de ces formes nues et estompées qui passaient et repassaient, besogneuses ou nonchalantes, qui se retenaient pour ne pas glisser, accrochées à des rampes imaginaires.

Ce nu-là était gîte, consolation et oubli de soi. Ce nu-là, alors invisible à mes yeux, déposait déjà dans ma tête l'impénétrable logique de ce qu'on montre et de ce qu'on cache, de ce qu'on étale et de ce qu'on subtilise, de ce qu'on cultive et de ce qu'on renie : le même corps, chez les mêmes femmes, à quelques heures d'intervalles.

Autres logiques du temps et de l'espace, du chaud et du froid, du clair et de l'obscur. Autres tenailles enserrant le beau et le laid, donnant son sel à la vie et sa nébulosité à l'existence.

Emna Bel Hadj Yahia
Ecrivain

Hammam

A chaque fois qu'Ella Douja, propriétaire du hammam, demandait mon âge, ma mère répondait que j'avais neuf ans - âge que j'ai du reste gardé trois ans durant - pour pouvoir prolonger l'accès à ce lieu exclusivement féminin.

Mahmoud Sehili
Peintre

Hammam, lieu de catharsis...

Dans ces labyrinthes de pierres polies par l'eau, la sueur et le souffle des corps baignants, la femme se débarrasse de ses voiles.
Son corps libre de toute contrainte se meut à son propre rythme, se perd dans le brouillard de vapeur, se noie sous une cascade d'eau vivifiante.
Lavée de toutes ses blessures cachées, elle se réconcilie avec elle-même et découvre qu'elle vibre autrement dans ce corps trop souvent mal «compris».

Aroussia Nallouti
Ecrivain

Hammam

 Je me souviens, quittant le hammam où j'accompagnais de très rares fois, mère, tante ou cousines, laissant derrière nous les éclats de voix et de rires des dernières baigneuses qui avaient du mal à s'arracher au ruissellement de la chaleur et de l'eau, que j'avais un souci.

En ce temps-là, et aujourd'hui encore je suppose, il y avait deux temps pour le même lieu : un temps pour les hommes et un temps pour les femmes. Et qui se succédaient.

Mon enfantin souci était que si ces femmes s'attardaient plus longtemps, surgiraient des «hommes», les étrangers par excellence, et surprendraient ces femmes insouciantes et abandonnées.

D'où venait cette crainte ? Etait-ce de l'audace de protéger de ces hommes les seins protecteurs ou du désir inconscient de ressurgir à leur place dans ce temps et ce lieu féminins, pour signifier à ces femmes ma frêle présence ?

J'ai l'impression qu'aujourd'hui certains de mes concitoyens tissent encore de leurs mains d'enfants attardés ce voile vaporeux entre les hommes et les femmes, pour continuer à se faire, peut-être délicieusement, peur.

Hamida Ben Ammar
Réalisateur

Hammam

Figurines

D'arcade en arcade la lumière traverse l'ombre. D'arcade en arcade la chaleur attrape les corps et devient suffocante tout à coup.

Les corps... la corpulence des uns se meut avec la finesse des autres. Les corps pleurent des larmes de sueur, se touchent, se succèdent à travers les allées de marbre mouillé...

Corps estompés dans des halos de vapeur, des corps ruisselants et mouvants.

Brillance ! ... Près du bassin d'eau fraîche, elles se désaltèrent à même la paume. Elles cueillent l'eau comme un fruit défendu.

Brillance ! des cheveux mouillés traversés d'étoiles... d'eau.Le bruit de l'eau est une musique, les cris des enfants peureux de cette multitude de corps nus accentuent l'écho... Odeur de sueur mêlée à l'odeur de savon, de shampoing, et... la mandarine qu'on effeuille comme une marguerite, branche de corail sortie des profondeurs marines ... une madeleine qui accompagne le café...

Fraîcheur et sueur, ombre et lumière, eau et pleurs des corps... multitude de corps jeunes et beaux, corps ronds, corps ridés, seins tristes parfois, seins fermes et tendus à l'appel de l'amour - eau claire et limpide, épousant la forme des corps comme des caresses lumineuses toujours renouvelées...

Les corps sont en fête, l'eau en cascade, et les cheveux dans l'attente. L'intimité se multiplie d'arcade en arcade, le bruit de l'eau compose l'harmonie et la lumière fugitive dévoile des estampes.

نافلة ذهب

Nefla Dhab
Ecrivain

Hammam

 C'est un espace qui me renvoie à l'enfance. J'y allais avec ma mère et toute la marmaille... Souvenir gai : circuler dans la vapeur, patauger dans l'eau, sortir bleu, ruisselant comme une éponge.

C'était une sortie, un voyage dans la forêt des corps.

Quand on grandit, ce lieu revêt une autre signification.

Dès l'âge de huit ans, je ne voulais plus y aller avec ma mère. Il n'y a pas que des belles choses à voir. Le hammam ne nous donne pas une image de l'harmonie. Je devenais un homme et n'avais plus besoin de ce lieu pour voir une jeune fille ou une femme nue.

Je suis traumatisé par le hammam. C'était au mois de Ramadan. Il y a vingt ans de cela, la veille de l'Aïd. Toutes les chambrettes étaient occupées, les masseurs aussi, l'eau ne suffisait pas. J'étais à jeun et j'ai dû attendre plus de trois heures. Complètement déshydraté, j'ai perdu connaissance. Pour sauver mon âme au jour du Jugement dernier, personne ne m'a donné une gorgée d'eau. J'ai quitté ce lieu dans un état lamentable.

Depuis ce jour, je suis allergique à la vapeur, à la chaleur et sujet à de vertiges. C'est dommage, mais je n'ai pas de regret.

Désormais, je me rends au hammam pour le plaisir de découvrir comment un peuple existe avec et dans son corps et... par esthétisme.

Mohamed DRISS
Homme de théâtre

Hammam

 Ecrivant, je prends conscience que Hammam se dit, s'écrit au masculin. En arabe et en français. Je le savais. Oui. Inconsciemment. Je le savais. J'ai dû si souvent l'écrire. Le parler. Sans penser. Au masculin.

Ecrivant aujourd'hui. Je prends conscience. Je le savais sans le savoir. Chaque fois que je visualise Hammam. Chaque fois que je remémore Hammam. Chaque fois me reviennent au corps et au cœur les bruits et les odeurs le chaud et le froid, l'ombre, la lumière et la pénombre, la moiteur la buée, le sec et le rêche des serviettes de bain, le doux glissement des vêtements frais sur le corps poli lisse.

Hammam. Enfance.

En moi vit, féminin, le hammam. Senti parlé chanté au féminin. Je la dis cette (mienne) réalité. Je la dis (je ne peux la dire qu') au féminin. Au premier (primaire ? pourquoi pas ?) degré. A fleur de corps et de cœur. Cœur et corps d'enfant. Enfant qui n'a pas encore (le fera-t-elle un jour ?) coupé le cordon ombilical. Ma mère. Hammam. Domaine de sa tendresse océane. Hammam qui la (ma mère) transformait en prêtresse d'un culte que je ne comprenais pas. Dont les rites fascinaient la fillette. Attendus. Espérés. Sans lesquels, parce qu'absente Elle, le hammam n'a plus son sens. Plus de sens.

Pourtant... Perdure le lieu. Perdurent les objets. Se répètent les gestes. Aujourd'hui. Inchangés ? Sans Elle.

Inéluctable désacralisation. Et irréversible. O temps. Abîme incomblé. Mais au tréfonds de l'être le hammam demeure ce temple de la purification toujours recommencée. Ce temple où pour la fillette aveugle aux autres, à leurs gestes, à leurs paroles, pour la fillette officie la Mère. Même cérémonial. Mêmes rites. Frappés d'un sceau unique. Gorgés d'un (plusieurs ?) sens. A Elle. Sens vécus sentis à fleur de cœur. Purification de l'amour d'Elle. Enveloppés dans les serviettes

de bain. Attente qu'Elle vienne. Elle, la dernière à sortir des chambres chaudes. Qu'elle vienne vers ses petits enveloppés dans les serviettes de bain. Qu'elle vienne à nous prendre place. Sa place. Près. Tout près. Attente délicieusement inconsciente. Attente du geste le baiser (encore chaud) de la purification accomplie. Du mot de bénédiction maternelle, le *saha* qui chante à jamais.

Hammam de mon enfance. Hammam de l'enfance.

Sophie El Goulli
Ecrivain

Hammam

 Evoquer l'atmosphère du hammam de mon enfance c'est d'abord et surtout me souvenir d'odeurs spécifiques et d'images presque surréalistes.

Vient l'odeur, c'est celle du *tfal*, argile noire qui nous vient du Maroc. Achetée en vrac au printemps et exposée au soleil dans des bacs en cuivre étamé, *kassaa*, elle est recouverte de géranium sauvage, de pétales de roses et de *zanzfoura* et diluée dans de l'eau de fleur d'oranger.

L'image, c'est celle du trousseau de la mariée, exposé dans le patio, à la veille du mariage. Parmi les paniers en osier, j'ai toujours été intrigué par la présence d'un récipient en cuivre jaune non martelé dans lequel trônait un sac en soie rempli de tfal.

C'est aussi celle, côté rue, d'un mulet, les yeux bandés qui tournait autour d'une noria sur la terrasse pour alimenter le hammam en eau.

C'est enfin l'image, à proximité de la porte d'entrée, du petit réduit souterrain, *fernak*, où le préposé au chauffage des bassins attisait le feu avec les copeaux ramassés chez les menuisiers du quartier.

Cette odeur de tfal parfumé, ce mulet qui dansait sur la terrasse au milieu d'un ballet de *foutas* multicolores balancées par le vent demeurent un souvenir vraiment inoubliable.

Ali Bellagha
Peintre

Hammam

Un Homme et trois Hammams

Le hammam des femmes figure dans ma mémoire comme un instant au croisement du plaisir, de la honte et de la colère.

Le hammam des hommes est par contre un moment morne et contraignant comme le réel.

Le hammam réinventé par l'enfant inconsolable que je demeure est un discours de séduction destiné à une femme de neige.

Moncef Dhouib

Hammam

Femmes voilées
portes closes
addition de sel et d'eau...
coule un ruisseau de vie
qui porte sur un visage de verdure
la traversée sera calme et bienfaisante
sur ce bateau aux voiles offertes
menant ces personnages en chair
femmes nues
clef du mystère
transparence du désir
cette eau qui s'écoule
arrose l'imaginaire
introduit le rêve.

Anouar Brahem
Musicien-compositeur

Hammam

 Je rêve aux hammams
Non pas à ces établissements «modernes» sans âme, où des corps esseulés subissent un espace moralement cellulaire. L'homme vient là, parmi de froides faïences et de vaines tuyauteries, revivre les plaisirs manqués de sa baignoire !

Je pense aux hammams d'antan, plongés dans une mystérieuse pénombre où la vie grouillante et colorée de la Médina et des faubourgs continue de respirer jusqu'au cœur surchauffé de ces lieux de grande convivialité.

Je pense aux murs épais de crépi dont la nudité accueillante veille sur des silhouettes abandonnées à la douce griserie d'un espace...

Aujourd'hui, les corps, toujours pressés, s'habillent sous l'acide lumière des néons qui rendent plus provocant le kitsch du décor et plus navrant le kitsch des âmes. Naguère, le temps devant soi, le temps pour soi, était une part d'éternité, et l'on ne s'avisait de tôt partir de crainte de compromettre la lente gestation d'un désir.

Les nouveaux hammams me rebutent. Des anciens me sépare le beau rêve de l'enfance. Si, d'aventure, je me retrouvais dans un de ces lieux où, autrefois, j'allais avec les amis comme au théâtre, pourrais-je sentir la même joie au cœur, le même frisson au corps ? Car les plus beaux hammams ne seraient-ils pas ceux, inaccessibles, où, désormais, l'on ne peut plus aller ?...

Ali Louati
Poète

44

Hammam

Tinte l'éternité
Je me fais comètes-femmes, bain turc
Cette eau si présente entre dunes
Et chemins sinueux, est diablesse
Femme dans l'instant aquatique

Lunes rougeoyantes
Devant l'essence de la flamme
Elle est mouvance
s'harmonisent les dissonances
L'herbe qui frappe
Les parfums sont des émissaires occultes
Penchés sur les lunes rougeoyantes
Le front du roc s'humecte
Flamme spectatrice, brassées de corps glissants
Les tintements s'écartent à l'extrême
La distance est jeu d'argile
Sueur invincible

فضيلة الشابي

Fadhila Chebbi
Poète

Traduit par Jean Fontaine

46

Hammam

«... et ta ville ne sera une ville vraiment parfaite que le jour où elle aura un hammam».

494ème nuit de Schéhérazade

 L'eau est la matière de l'imagination par excellence et la reine purificatrice. De l'impur au pur, le hammam se fait le support de l'imaginaire où le corps se trouve en harmonie parfaite avec la terre et l'eau. Le rapport corporel avec la matière dont on s'enduit, forge cette expérience : terre revitalisante et féconde où les rêves et les parfums riches, onctueux - mélange de jasmin, de santal, d'ambre, de girofle et de laurier-aphrodisiaques... le regard, le toucher, donnent au corps sa véritable dimension. La beauté est là atteinte par cette volupté thermique eau - feu - corps : union durable.

Humidité chaude, humidité froide associées à un monde intérieur dissimulé dans les épaisseurs de l'être... passage d'une sensation à une autre afin de parvenir à l'extrême désir de l'expérience sensuelle. Là, le corps et le lieu font que l'espace social devient pouvoir.

Succession de passages qui se réduit spatialement à une organisation architecturale simple. Par sa nature, ce lieu devient créatif, poétique où l'histoire se confond avec le moi et les autres, avec le moi et les parfums; mon moi, pur, simple, laid, magique, magnifique, aquatique, là où réside toute notre histoire de la Méditerranée.

Lotfi Ben Abderrazak
Architecte

عثمان
الفضروي

Hammam

Etrange sensation que celle qui nous envahit au hammam : la chaleur active la circulation du sang, s'empare de l'esprit et de l'imagination...

La rupture avec l'espace et le temps profanes s'accomplit. Le hammam, temple du corps pur et propre du citadin musulman, se transforme en un lieu onirique, un lieu d'hallucinations, de rêve, où l'imagination est reine, où l'on s'évade loin, très loin dans des univers mystérieux où la volonté et le social disparaissent derrière ce rideau opaque de vapeur, l'oubli... où l'on se sent si près de soi, si près de son corps, de sa nudité, où l'on se sent pour quelques heures appartenir à nulle part, où l'on se sent aller, confiante, soumise, heureuse.

نَاكِي بُوشْرَارَةُ ٱلزَّنَّاد

Traki Bouchrara Zannad
Sociologue

Hammam

A l'orée du bain... regards zébrés d'azur

Ce bassin étoilé où tu t'es immergée, flottante (l'image d'un temps à la mesure de l'eau qui monte en moi), se creuse en des trous éplorés. La peau de liquide fumant qui t'entoure, te noie, t'enfonce, j'y tombe comme un pavé et l'eau fascinée t'enferme comme une trappe d'argent. En te regardant dans ton écran transparent, je me suis mieux vu et je ne pourrai jamais l'oublier.

Vénus naissant de la rosée, portée par les effluves de musc et de jasmin, l'eau est ton voile ; ta peau appelle au vertige ta chair irisée.

Ta nudité, la moiteur entêtante, le lourd encens, mettent mon regard et mon cœur en émoi ; tu fascines et tu émerveilles.

A la poursuite de ton odeur, de tes formes et de tes contours montrés avec une tranquille insouciance, ta beauté est une exigence autant spirituelle qu'esthétique. Je pourrais te regarder à en perdre la vue, te caresser au delà de l'usure, couler à tes lèvres l'eau de mes rêves, connaître toutes tes saveurs, suivre du doigt le tracé de tes veines.

Cachée - dévoilée, ombre et lumière, femme surprise dans sa nudité, tu ne peux te soustraire à ma contemplation ravisseuse dans ce lieu, ventre féminin. Le bain, espace du non-dit, où tout se sait et se voit. Ce bain, qui respirait avec nous le bonheur par ses murs et ses étuves, comme autant de bouches entrouvertes, d'où montaient des haleines de vie.

Ma créature alanguie, mon odalisque, mon «fantasme-oriental», ma transparente et diaprée, l'eau est le rets indiscret de ta volupté. Des éclaboussures de lumière à en devenir aveugle.

Dans ton bain donnant sur le port antique, devant les coquillages venus de rivages oubliés, tu te regardais dans le miroir, étudiant ton meilleur effet et tu m'imaginais. Tu te recomposais un visage souriant ou fermé. Un visage qui passe dans la foule et se fixe dans mon regard.

Perverse, tu connaissais l'existence de ta nudité dérobée et comment pourrais-je t'oublier et te remercier pour ce que tu es, pour ce que tu m'as donné malgré toi ?

Hantés par le désir de te voir, les regards sont voleurs, à la surface même de l'œuvre et traverse l'écran de toutes les apparences.

Femme au bain, je crois pouvoir te dire, que d'aucun instant, d'aucune respiration, d'aucune palpitation, tu n'es absente.

Rachid Koraïchi
Peintre

Hammam

Il suffirait de presque rien... pour qu'enfin tu scintilles. Mais la mer est loin, elle qui pourtant se re-tient aux portes de la ville et des alcôves.

Murs gonflés d'eau, boursouflés d'humidité et de silences. *Balyouns* cerclés de fer, lourds à porter. Leur bois prend l'eau. Ils n'arpenteront jamais le large. Il suffirait de crever le ciel pour que l'eau exulte, mais la mer est loin et les mots sont des cercles premiers.

«Ne reste jamais seule dans le hammam, disait-elle, des créatures y circulent. Il est des trésors cachés et la cupidité est sans scrupules... Ne reste jamais seule dans le hammam, la *Nhaïssa* pourrait s'ouvrir...»

Mais les corps qui déambulent, nimbés de sueur et de brouhaha, sont si loin du clair, si près de l'obscur. Brûleraient-ils leurs chandelles par les deux bouts, certains soirs de saphir ?

«Ne romps jamais les scellés, disait-elle, tu éclaterais comme une bulle. Le cristal est traître et les amants se renient un jour».

Mais c'est pour moi que sonnent les clairons du bleu et c'est à tes pieds que mon eau se brise.

Splendeur de l'eau qui roule pour qu'il y ait enfin tonnerre. La mer souffle par tes narines : bruis... il restera toujours de ton sel quelque chose.

«Ne pleure pas dans tes rêves, disait-elle, tous les enfants grandissent». La terre est cendre mais ton pouls sera ma voix, tant que tu vivras. Ne pleure pas dans tes rêves, tes sanglots remuent mon sommeil et mes draps. Ne me pleure pas, qui a dit que l'eau est mortelle ?»

Tous les enfants grandissent et sur ta peau, le sel vrille comme mon ivresse. Ce glaive est ma cascade malgré son double tranchant...
Et je ne cesse de frémir et de brunir pour tes doigts, oublieuse des êtres et des objets semés au hasard des villes et des paris incompris.

Tunis, La Saint-Valentin de l'an mil neuf cent quatre-vingt douze.

Alia Tabaï
Ecrivain

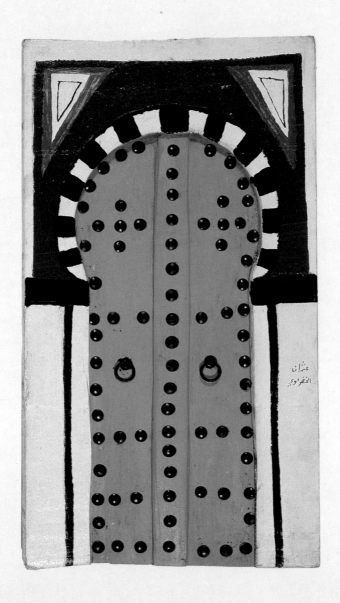

Hammam

 La société musulmane est fondée sur la stricte séparation des sexes. Le Hammam, s'il est un lieu de purification, est également un lieu social où cette règle n'est pas toujours respectée d'une manière rigoureuse. Quand le hammam est ouvert aux hommes, aucune femme, aucune fillette n'y est admise. Il n'en est pas de même lorsque le hammam est ouvert aux femmes. Aucun homme adulte n'y est certes admis mais les garçons le sont.

La règle y est d'admettre avec les femmes les enfants non pubères. Mais cette règle elle-même n'est que théorique. L'âge de la puberté n'étant pas le même pour tous les individus, il ne saurait fournir qu'une limite élastique et lâche. Comme une mère a tendance à voir dans son fils un éternel enfant, comme au surplus mener un garçon au hammam est une corvée dont le père préfère se décharger - aussi longtemps que possible - sur la mère, le spectacle de grands enfants, de pré-adolescents admis au hammam avec les femmes n'est pas rare. C'est même la source de «scandales» quotidiens, tellement quotidiens qu'on n'y fait plus attention, sauf si notre jeune adolescent se laisse aller à des gestes déplacés ou à des paroles peu pudiques. C'est alors l'expulsion...

L'enfant ira dorénavant au hammam des hommes : c'est comme un rite d'initiation au monde mâle. La conduite du hammam va se structurer de manière nouvelle pour lui au moment même où il est ôté à sa mère. Le hammam va être pour lui à la fois une consécration, une confirmation et une compensation : n'a-t-il pas été rejeté et parfois même de manière violente du hammam des femmes ? Mais en même temps, le hammam va être pour lui comme un retour imaginaire au monde ancien. Comment ne sera-t-il pas lié pour lui à des fantasmes d'enfance? N'est-ce pas le lieu où il a accompagné tant de fois sa mère, ses sœurs, ses cousines, où il a rencontré maintes et maintes fois en tenue d'Eve les charmantes voisines ?

A. W. Bouhdiba

Extrait de la Revue Tunisienne des Sciences Sociales, n°1, septembre 1966

Glossaire

Aïd : fête
Asfour stah : oiseau des terrasses.
Balyoun : seau en bois.
Doukkana : banquette en bois ou en pierre qui se trouve dans le vestiaire du hammam.
Fernak : fourneau où l'on chauffe l'eau qui alimente le hammam.
Fouta : serviette du hammam
Gehenne : enfer dans les écrits bibliques.
Halfaouine : quartier nord de la Médina de Tunis.
Hammam : bain de vapeur public ou bain maure.
Harza : employée au hammam des femmes qui, munie d'un gant rêche «kassa», frictionne la peau pour en détacher la saleté et s'occupe de la cliente pendant la durée du bain.
Henné : teinture rouge obtenue à partir d'un arbuste dont les feuilles séchées et moulues donnent une poudre verte parfumée. Mélangée à l'eau elle devient une pâte brune qui sert à teindre les cheveux, les mains et les pieds des femmes à l'occasion des mariages et est censée les protéger du mauvais œil.
Kouttab : école coranique.
Lablabi : soupe de pois chiche.
Medina : ville traditionnelle arabe.
Nhassa : grande marmite où chauffe l'eau du hammam
Noria : machine à godets permettant de puiser de l'eau.
Quattous : littéralement, le chat. Ce mot désigne aussi la fièvre, la bouffée trop abondante de vapeur.
Saha : parole que l'on prononce à la sortie du bain et qui signifie «que le bain te soit bénéfique».
Sefsari : voile dans lequel s'enveloppent les femmes.
Tassaa : vase de cuivre à long manche.
Tayeb : masseur dans le hammam des hommes.
Tfal : argile réduite en pâte et appliquée sur le corps en guise de savon.
Zanzfoura : fleur de tilleul.

Maquette : May ANGELI

Réalisation : Promotion Services
Impression : Imprimeries Réunies
Groupe Cérès Productions
6, Avenue Abderrahman Azzam - 1002 Tunis
Tél : 282.033
Novembre 1992